MEDIUMSHIP TOUCHING THE STARS

EILEEN DAVIES

In Memory of all pioneers of 'truth'

Voiceless.......saffron lanterns,

Float.....in the dark grief of sky.

Tracing a path to the stars.

Even in death,

You thought of those left behind.

So.....much so.

You lit a trail of love,

To light the way.

CONTENTS

CONTENTS

CHAPTER SIX

Our Rich and Diverse Heritage - 111

CHAPTER SEVEN

Practical Suggestions - 139

INTRODUCTION

The divine mystery silently weaves its design and binds the unseen threads of each life one with the other, each strand intricately inter-twined. Even those we have never actually met can have an influence upon the unfolding pattern of our lives..

I owe my being here, as do my other family members, to the captain of a Royal Navy ship, someone I never knew, who passed to the spirit some years before I was born. During the second world war my father was enlisted to serve onboard a ship, to cover for someone granted sick leave who held the position of a radio telegraphist. This role he fulfilled for some months until, when the person returned, my father asked the captain if he could be granted permission to stay onboard and continue within his assigned job. The captain's reply was 'no', much to my father's surprise, his reason being that my father was not on the original role list and the captain did not believe in 'tampering with fate'. Consequently, my father was sent off to serve on board another vessel, but these words proved to be fatalistic indeed, as the next mission saw the ship being torpedoed and sunk, without one survivor!

My father's life had been spared due to the foresight and superstitious disposition of the captain. Yet there were times when beneath the light-hearted humour that he so often showed to the world, a sadness would silently steal across his face and a faraway look glaze his vision. It was as if he was recalling those earlier days and the ghost of his past haunted the silent places within, as past ghosts must do in the lives of all those who served their country in war and have fought other men's battles. My father survived the second world war despite being at times engaged in dangerous missions; his destiny to return from it was sealed.

I have in my possession an old penny which is miss-shaped by the impact of a bullet that saved the life of a friend of my father. A humble penny in his pocket, which gave far more than its value at the time by preventing what could have potentially been fatal consequences from a bullet heading his way; thankfully the bullet didn't have my father's or his friend's name on it and once more another life was spared. It seemed the universe was conspiring to make certain of some people's survival and that they would return to a normal life again when the clouds of war dispersed.

The implications of such stories remind us of the fragility of human existence but also the remarkable synchronicities which serve to take us deeper into realms of human experience and allow us to ponder the reasons and the 'whys'.

A story enables the mind to journey on a voyage of wonder and exists as an invitation to embrace the miraculous even when true, for it has the capacity to bypass the intellect and unite the head and the heart in the same moment. Our lives are made of stories; droplets of moments that make up each individual life as each page is turned and each chapter written, what divine possibilities and wonders are there for those who have the vision to really see. The invisible threads that unknowingly unite all in the great mystery. If any one of us were absent the divine harmony would be incomplete.

This gives rise to the question of whether there is such a thing as destiny or fate. Is there really a divine plan of which we are all a part? Does the very meaning of life have deeper implications and what will survive of us when we die? Is there really a time to be born and a time to die? To any thinking person all these questions surely arise in our consciousness throughout the various changing circumstances which constitute our lives.

Retrospect enlarges our vision and sometimes it's not until we have reached the later years that as we look back on our life, we can perceive a pattern which wasn't always apparent at the time, when confronted with the challenges life frequently presents.

As a child, like many mediums, I kept the company of spirit children. I was frequently seen speaking to invisible friends, much to the concern of my parents. It's hard to describe the reality with which I entered my spirit 'playground' and how in my childish mind there was never any doubt as to the authenticity of the presence of my friends. But looking back it is somewhat strange, as on occasion I would see the spirit children in full and at other times it was as though they built up in my awareness, starting at the feet until the whole body formed. At the time it seemed perfectly usual; I suppose children have no comparison and it was all I had ever known. Even to this day I still have a very clear memory of how my spirit friends looked and how they made me feel. The vivid recollection of being loved and accepted just for being who I am remains as an echo within me.

Rudolf Steiner maintained that children live in and through their spiritual senses until around the age of seven. It was his vision to encourage the natural ability inherent in children through education, for them to live in their imaginative selves nurturing an ability to draw from a creative power of the soul, forging a strong connection with the earth and the natural rhythm of the seasons. He believed it was the very foundation of being and the only way to ensure, as a child becomes an adult, that there would be a harmony between spirit, body, and mind with feet firmly planted on the earth, but gaze fixed upon the heavens. Steiner said, "Our highest endeavour must be to develop human beings who are able to impart purpose and direction to their lives. The need for imagination, a sense of truth and a feeling of responsibility".

I recall with great clarity one day when I had been outside playing with a friend who lived in a house across the road my mother asking me on my return if I knew any African children, as a little girl of African appearance wearing a red dress had knocked at our door asking if I wanted to play. I must add at this point in time in the area where I lived there were no African children in the neighbourhood. This was an epiphany moment for me, as this experience occurred just at the same time as I was awakening to the realisation that no one else seemed to be able to see the spirit friends who I sometimes shared my life with.

Questions arose excitedly in my mind and I felt that now my mother would know that I wasn't imagining these friends and they were real. It was a short time after this that my two spirit friends seemed to disappear, but maybe my African friend Ulla's visit was enough in some way to relay much needed reassurance. I remember sitting in the room where I so frequently played with my two spirit friends and no one appeared. All the wishing of a child's heart could not summon or make them visible, not for one moment. Interestingly, it was at around the age of seven that my abilities to see the spirit friends disappeared. I felt bereft and they left a space in my heart; during the passage of time this grief began to fade, although the memory remained, as I became immersed in all that occupies the ordinary life of a child, if the life of anyone can be labelled as ordinary.

A few years later a family from Africa actually moved into the neighbourhood, needless to say I immediately had a great liking for them. There was a familiarity within their vibrancy and the bright colours they wore that reminded me of my now vanished spirit companion Ulla, and from time to time I would fleetingly question her absence.

Looking back, I must have been a bit of an enigma to my parents, with strange questions such as 'if God exists then who made God?'. At an early age I pondered upon life and had an annoying habit of seeing lights moving in the atmosphere around people, the colours spoke to me through the language of thought and feelings often making me wary of certain people, other times at ease. I would tell stories of past lives to my friends and recall faraway lands, memories of other lives were like a present reality within me. But I also vividly remember being scolded by my friend's mother for telling lies. The world was indeed a very difficult place to be as a child simply sharing the stories I knew to be real.

Once my recently passed cat appeared as though through the window and jumped onto my bed and in his normal habit, settled down beside me. Every other night when going to bed I would see faces looming up to me in my inner vision; so real were the faces some gaunt and thin, others smiling and happy, that I used to be afraid of going to sleep in case the faces would appear. I would hear names being called and voices in languages I didn't always understand. The spirit voices were very clear, yet as I look back must have been subjective, as no one else seemed to hear the voices I so often heard in the stillness of my room. Such is the connection which children can naturally experience when living from a place of innocence, not yet having lost touch with their spiritual senses, until the memory of our spiritual home begins to fade and living in this material world takes over. Gradually our childhood otherworldliness evaporates, creating an absence of what was once a natural state of being.

In my early teens I lived a life which was considered normal for my age. Yet my connection with the spirit world, even though more subtle, never really left me. On my journey home from school, I often felt compelled to stop by the quintessentially Anglian church at the end of the road where we lived. I remember the distinct contrast I always felt, from the outside world, as I opened the heavy oak door. It was like entering another reality, the atmosphere seemed to be imbued with the hopes and prayers of those who had been there before me. The air inside often hung heavy with clouds of residual incense and soft diffused light would create myriad colours as it shone through the stained-glass windows onto the aged floor.

On reflection, I believe much of my mediumistic development was deepened within its stone walls. I had never heard of the word meditation or knew what it meant, yet it felt natural to me to close my eyes and absorb the quiet power that permeated the atmosphere as I entered a sense of timelessness and peace, which sustained me in a way I didn't quite comprehend at the time. I preferred the church when it was empty of people, as the language of silence conveyed far more than any spoken word ever could. In addition I couldn't conceive a concept of God that was portrayed by the scriptures, as they didn't seem to embody much in the way of all that was holy and sacred; I failed to grasp how any newly born baby could be born in sin, after all a few gurgles and burps didn't amount to much in the way of sin, in any man's language!

I can't pretend that I was aware of those in the spirit world at this point in my life, yet a preoccupation with the supernormal intrigued me. However, I did have a very strange occurrence, when I had to take an important maths test, the results of which would determine the level of class, I would be placed in. I had an intense dislike of maths and it was most definitely not my favourite subject, I did not understand the world of equations and fractions, so I decided it might be a good idea, to invent a good excuse why I couldn't go to school that particular day! Feeling suitably pleased with the fact I had missed the dreaded test; I happily went to school the following day thinking I had been saved. Unfortunately, the Head of the Maths Department thought otherwise and I was consequently ushered into an empty room, under his watchful presence. I distinctly recall the uncomfortable feeling I had in the pit of my stomach; I could hardly make any sense of the questions let alone provide any answers! I had to escape from this stressful situation, so I proceeded to write down any number that floated into my head, no calculations, no working out, just a random answer. Test completed I placed it upon his desk, with a sense of freedom and relief, after all what did it matter? I wasn't planning on a career; that would be dependent on my mathematical skills anyway!

The next day, I got called into the Head of the Maths department's office, apparently, I was a complete mystery, I had achieved a remarkable 95%! it was as much a shock to me, as it was the teacher, as it was generally known that maths was not one of my strengths; but I had no explanation as to how I had arrived at such accurate answers and I needed one!

Years later, Ulla told me that she had dropped the correct answers in my mind, as she had an awareness of my deep distress and wanted to help.

Another teacher at my secondary school, shared a story of 'a near death experience' she had encountered after a very serious car accident. The accident left her permanently disabled. Yet rather than be bitter, she conveyed a tangible peace, that was never present before. What struck me the most was not just her fascinating account of the event and how she had met her father who had passed some years before, but just how much it had changed her personality for the better. It was without doubt a complete transformation.

I also recall the same teacher saying that "a baby, has to learn how to smile and doesn't smile until the memory of the world, which it had come from had been forgotten".

Years later, I was to receive the most extraordinary proof of the truth of those spirit friends, through the remarkable mediumship of Gordon Higginson, the then President of the Spiritualists National Union, Gordon's incredible abilities covered the breadth and depth of all mediumistic powers. I received with astounding accuracy validation of my earlier childhood days, sitting by his side along with another colleague in the library at the Arthur Findlay College. Through the gift of trance communication and delivered with humour from a spirit helper called 'Paddy', who was known for breath-taking accuracy, any doubt regarding proof of my spirit friends was wiped from my mind as information was conveyed that no other living person knew. My heart skipped a beat, it was extraordinary; there was the spirit with great clarity giving me confirmation of thoughts that had arisen in my mind just two weeks prior to going to the college and my questions were answered! Could the other world read our thoughts and to what depths did they know all about us? From childhood days to present, with swift accuracy, including the name of the street where I had lived as a child, all was disclosed in a manner in which only I had known the significance and meaning. The proof I was privileged to experience that warm summer's day stayed with me the rest of my life as a reminder of the intelligence of those in the unseen world.

This was not the only proof of the certain reality of my childhood spirit friends, as years later on one occasion when working with a dear friend and colleague, Glyn Edwards, I was given a spirit drawing from someone I had never met before. I received a portrait of a beautiful African woman, so amazingly drawn of my spirit friend Ulla; no longer in the form of a child yet still recognisable, as so many of us are when an older version of our younger selves.

The third proof came in the form of a seance held in my home town. I had been teaching on a course shared with the extraordinary physical medium Scott Milligan. In the afternoon I had given a demonstration of trance mediumship where my spirit influence had given a talk ending with a reference to one of the people present that was somewhat light-hearted. This was quite unusual as normally the spirit teachers don't really make much in the way of personal comments to individual people, their message is usually directed to everyone present as a whole. No word of this was mentioned to Scott, who at the time was resting. During the seance with Scott that same evening Ulla spoke through independent direct voice (a form of physical mediumship) and proceeded to finish a conversation she had begun earlier in the day in the demonstration of trance. Amusingly, I was not spoken to at all which was funny considering I was her medium and that we worked as part of a team. However, the evidence was fascinating considering all the facts and how much effort must have gone into the co-ordination of communication, in order to convince myself and others present that, apart from our spirit loved ones, those we call our spirit helpers or friends are just as much real and not a figment of our imagination or wishful thinking.

Although my father lived to survive the war years, he passed when I was just a teenager and it was his very passing which led me on my search for proof and ultimately to the doorway of spiritualism, as bereavement has done with so many others. The experience kindled an innate desire to seek confirmation of something I felt strongly within my own heart and knew to be true; that the person I loved was still alive out of sight maybe, but his deepest essence, his spirit, lived on.

My father's passing was the catalyst for change and sent my life spinning in a new direction as the following year I moved from the south of England, up and across the border to bonnie Scotland. I remember travelling by train on what seemed the longest journey one could ever take, as my mind was filled with the uncertainty of leaving all I had ever known and was familiar with behind. The unknown loomed like a cloud above me. The passing miles seemed to take forever. It was the month of October and one year exactly since my father had left this world and my heart was heavy with loss, from the space he once filled and the love of the people I was leaving behind.

As the train began to draw nearer to Aberdeen and the lights of the city sparkled in the distance, I wondered what my future fate would be and about the people I had not yet met, but whose lives might be mysteriously entwined with my own. Arriving in autumn, to cold winds and the pungent aroma of fish from Aberdeen's then thriving fish markets, my heart sank. Why did I ever agree to the idea of moving and what was the purpose? All my original plans to continue my life down south had evaporated before me at the very last minute and now here I was standing at a station feeling far from home. It may as well have been halfway across the world; the accents of everyone speaking around me seemed like a completely foreign language to a girl from southern England.

In retrospect I feel those lights I had seen on nearing the city were a symbolic reflection of the light of the spirit world, guiding my pathway unknowingly in a direction that was instrumental in providing immensely supportive and grounded spiritual development, where I was privileged to have contact with some of the greats of spiritualism, those who were the most respected in their field and whose lives were a testimony to all they held dear. I feel privileged that my journey has been influenced by people who were outstanding and the very greatest ambassadors to those in the world unseen. The wonderful Gordon Higginson, Eric and Heather Hatton, Glyn Edwards. Like lanterns illuminating the way, these remarkable people remain a powerful presence in the lives of all they knew, as though they were still here. Had the timing been different and my road another path, I may never have been blessed to experience their close support and encouragement. And so the fabric of our lives is woven, by invisible threads and unseen hands.

Were a star quenched on high,

For ages would its light,

Still travelling downward from the sky,

Shine on our mortal sight.

So, when a great man dies,

For years beyond our ken

The light he leaves behind him lies

Upon the paths of men.

Henry Wadsworth Longfellow.

I copied down this very touching poem when I gifted a book to Gordon during the last of his many visits to Aberdeen, a few weeks before he passed to the spirit world. Although it seemed strange, I felt strongly impressed to do so. I worried considerably about this afterwards, after all it was more or less telling someone they were going to pass. What would he think? But it proved to be the last time I would see him, this side of life anyway, as five weeks later he passed. The inner self knows how we should listen to heart intuition in a way the head cannot always comprehend. The words of this poem proved to be prophetic in many ways, not only for Gordon's imminent passing but in just how much his presence and his teachings still touch the paths of those who have never met him and are influenced by his light regardless. But then, when he was born, those great souls in the spirit world chose to give him the spirit name of light.

Sometimes life calls to us of the need to believe in things we can neither see nor touch, yet we receive far more than we could ever imagine by the very grace of belief. After all we can't see love, yet it is the whole meaning and purpose of existence.

CHAPTER ONE

MEDIUMSHIP A THRESHOLD TO AWAKENING

_____   _____

"Learn to acknowledge your birth right, the power that created the stars

in all their glory and the flowing rivers, has crowned your consciousness

with the vision to behold wonder and your heart to know love so the

song of the universe may flow through your veins and the miracle of

creation know the splendour of your praise".

Trance teachings.

Mediumship is a means to comprehend a larger life, a vaster reality beyond the confines of everyday awareness and limited vision, where we can stand on tiptoe and touch the stars.

The two most fundamentally important qualities that should be developed when considering exploring any mediumistic potential is to first, learn the ability to listen with our whole self and secondly, to love with all of our heart.

Mediumistic awareness is as much about the discovery of our own self and our true nature as it is the ability to communicate with other realms. At the very least it enriches our perception and is the illumination of the soul where we learn to engage with life through human experience and glimpse the eternal. Within the soul there is a hidden elsewhere, it is the soul's divine longing to know itself through the language of love and the remembrance of our eternal home.

Attempting to describe mediumistic experience, however, brings its own limitations and challenges. In every sense and meaning of the word communication between the different dimensions is a dichotomy, for by its very nature is nebulous and intangible, yet at the same time is incredibly real. It's as though mediumship is a process which functions in the twilight of reality. Beyond the boundaries which are created by a need to clothe experience with words, there exist realms of heightened awareness to explore. Although within this state there are areas of shared commonality, it is ultimately unique to the individual. Poet and mystic William Blake once said, "everything though appears without is really within". This aptly applies to mediumship; it is our inner spiritual abilities that enable each of us to commune with other worlds. Each person expresses as great a level of spiritual power as he has the capacity to receive.

Mankind has undoubtedly always communed with higher powers and with those who have departed this physical world. It is certainly by no means a new faculty; prophets, seers, mystics, poets and artists, the list is long, have all experienced an awareness of other realities that, once encountered, have caused a transformation in their being. Their legacy is all they have gifted to the world in their various creative forms. A divine interpretation and testimony of their experience, which for them was spontaneous and unrehearsed.

In the past, access to higher realms of consciousness was only for a few rare souls, who through their devotion and spirituality had earned the right to experience divine revelations and manifestation of spiritual powers.

A trend has emerged, in more recent times, to develop once hidden aspects of human nature. Mediumship is fast becoming the norm in our modern world and through the media has become popularised.

True mediumship is a natural process and implies a deepening of receptivity creating expansion in awareness, a momentary leaving behind of all worldly perception. The ability I believe is inherent in all people as, essentially, we are all spiritual beings, it's just with some people the ability is a little nearer the surface than with others. A medium, it can be said, forms a bridge of consciousness for those who have not yet developed their sensitivity enough to communicate for themselves.

Reality exists beyond our sensory perception, there can be no doubt. The splitting of the atom by Ernest Rutherford, back in 1917, gave birth to a dawning of a new wave of thought concerning the nature of the universe. Remarkably, pre-dating this in 1909, two Theosophists, A. Besant and C. W. Leadbeater, using their Yogic and clairvoyant powers and a term they called 'shrinking perception' described the nature and structure of matter and atomic particles. They even went so far as to describe all 92 naturally occur-ring elements down to the quark and sub-quark correctly. The last quark in the atom wasn't discovered until as recently as 1995! And yet Besant and Leadbeater mentioned them a remarkable 78 years ahead of the world of science! Extraordinary, indeed; surely then the question that must arise in the mind of any thinking person is, just how was this even possible? Little do we realise the vast reservoir of untapped potential which lies waiting to be discovered within us all, for many we are just scratching the surface!

Even more phenomenal is the fact that in the thirteenth century, the Persian mystic and Sufi scholar Jalaluddin Rumi, in his ecstatic states when performing his devotional whirling, uttered timeless truths in the most poetic language. In his divinely inspired utterances Rumi describes 'an elemental universe in which atoms dance driven by love'. Maybe the scientifically minded researchers may come yet to discover that love is indeed the missing key. Although it fails to fit into a scientific formula, love is written upon the soul, in the handwriting of the divine and is the substance of life itself and love, or want of it, has been the source of every creative expression known to man.

Our world is not as it would appear to the uninitiated or unaware. For the invisible sustains the visible and there exist worlds of consciousness to explore, if we but knew. As one ancient Rishi (Rishi being a Sanskrit term for a person who, after intense meditation of the Vedas, realizes supreme truth) named Vasishta said, "infinite worlds come and go in the vast expanse of my consciousness, they are like motes of dust dancing in a beam of light". The building blocks of our universe are atoms, which are nothing other than a cosmic dance of transient energy and empty space. Why then should we even begin to deny other realities exist, that consciousness survives bodily death and the truth that communication between the two realms of existence is not only possible but factual. The question we must ask ourselves is what do we miss, if we do not believe?

The quality of thought determines our lives and how we perceive reality. What we experience is collectively shaped by our unconscious beliefs, we live in the thought generation of the past and have unfortunately inherited the conditioning created by our ancestors. We do not see things as they really are but as we are predetermined to see them and frequently fail to ask ourselves, "what do I believe?".

Our mediumistic powers are revealed when we begin, layer by layer, to remove all the labels and conditioning that stop us from recognising them as an inherent part of our intrinsic nature. We are beings of limitless potential, the power within is not only eternal but divine. The door to higher perception is opened through self-inquiry. Who is the self, who exactly is it that perceives? Can we discern the presence behind thinking, is our true nature uncovered once we do this? The more we have become immersed in intellectualizing and thinking, the more we identify with the ego to the detriment of the spirit.

Mediumistic awakening then requires an understanding of who we really are and calls us to respond by cultivating a spiritual attitude. For with the revealing of mediumistic powers comes enormous responsibility and an opportunity to serve humanity, to enhance the life of one person means to benefit the whole. The role of mediumship should be to bring the soothing balm of comfort to the bereaved and to lead mankind to the threshold of truth. A truth which if fully embraced can be the source of both inner and outer transformation.

To view the world through the window of awareness broadens our vision, until we no longer see from a limited perspective, but view the whole. As the poet Ella Wheeler Wilcox (1850-1919) so aptly conveys in her poem, '

Progress

Let there be many windows in your soul

That all the glories of the universe

May beautify it. Not the narrow pane

Of one poor creed can catch the radiant rays.

That shine from countless sources. Tear away the binds of superstition;

Let the light; pour through fair windows broad as truth itself

And high as God.

We need to begin to see the bigger picture and claim ownership of our life. Every time one person finds a new way to respond in a peaceful, positive manner, the greater whole receives the benefit. Our world mirrors collective response, if we focus on the inner rather than the outer, we help quicken our own spiritual awareness, which ultimately affects the evolutionary progress of mankind.

We live in a multi-dimensional universe and are ourselves multi-dimensional beings, capable of much more than we could ever realise. If we can dream it, we can do it, but first we must learn to transcend our conditioning and all the outdated fear-based thinking which has restricted past generations. In our thinking we must be free, by doing so we will maximise our potential, which for too long we have denied.

Humanity has finally begun to awaken from a long sleep, and at last endeavours to wipe the dust away from our eyes so we can begin to see clearly and claim ownership of our divine heritage, consequently enabling each one of us to potentially reach a new stage in evolution. We have now developed the capacity to conceive God as an inner reality and recognise this creative power as an intrinsic part of our own being, by so doing we have progressed from 'knowing about God' and replaced this with 'knowing God', a direct experience within. A far distant cry from the sun or idol worship era of primitive man, advancement on all levels of understanding is taking place, at accelerating rates. Look how every month technological understanding surpasses itself and is reformed anew. In the process of evolution, consciousness has become conscious of itself. We have travelled far to reach the place we are now at in the great circle of life but what are we to do with this newly discovered knowledge for to know is one thing, to act upon is another.

We wouldn't even be here if it wasn't for the countless souls who have helped us in our life, both consciously and unconsciously, in more ways than we could ever care to imagine. Yet we can only understand life by fully entering into it and by the art of allowing ourselves to be fully present to ourselves. Learning to train the mind in the art of being concerned with the now, this present moment matters as this is all we ever really have.

The age we are now living in beckons each one of us to learn to live direct from our own centre of wholeness and authenticity of the spirit and to foster a new way of being. This by consequence is taking spirituality to the market-place of life by measure of availability and choice, creating an opportunity to explore, what has been in the past, areas of human nature which have been neglected, except for those rare people who have responded to the inner voice to seek a life of service and devotion to God. There exists within each of us the wisdom of the spirit, which differs greatly from knowledge. For knowledge can alter with the light of new knowledge, but wisdom is a perennial stream that is changeless and timeless. In the past we have discovered knowledge but failed to realise wisdom. We need to experience unity in our thinking; by doing this one thing we have the capacity to transform our life. If it is true that we are shaped by our thoughts, it must follow then that if we concentrate on purifying our minds, joy will emerge like the sun, which always shines.

It is important to ask ourselves, what can I give back to life? How will my being here benefit another? Is there some unique quality, which will serve to enhance and enrich in anyway, however great or small? We all have something to offer life, a reason for being alive. Maybe we just need to attune ourselves in such a way that we do not miss the very reason why we are here. It is imperative to add life to our days, not days to our life. I am sure the question we will ask ourselves at the end of earthly life will be 'how much did I love'?

The wisdom which was expressed in the life of the Anthroposophist and visionary Rudolf Steiner conveys the significance of spiritual responsibility, for in his lifetime's works he emphasised how important it is to pay attention to the inner life, for every two steps you take towards higher development you must take four towards self-development. The cultivation of heightened powers of awareness alone is not enough, we should work towards developing ourselves as spiritual beings. The effects of which will surely last throughout eternity. What greater benefit could we possibly achieve?

Mediumship then, cannot be developed in isolation but should go hand in hand with efforts to spiritualise the self, like two threads of twine intricately woven together that visibly appear as one. Religion frequently divides, but spirituality by contrast unites. It supersedes the boundaries created by any one path and embraces the whole. Every religion has at its heart love, but love has no religion. Love is of course a universal language that transcends the spoken word and the barriers created by culture or class. What if inter-spirituality is the new religion of the future, a future where we revere all life and recognise wherever we tread as sacred and holy ground. Surely it would enrich us to aspire towards a standard of living where spiritual awareness is an organic process, an integral part of our life, whereby the word religion is replaced by 'a way of life'; one that is morally, ethically and spiritually inspired. This could be the meeting place where all unite, a brotherhood is possible if we teach children the beauty in diversity and try to cultivate unity. Teach them that different does not necessarily mean wrong, rather than continue with outdated sectarian beliefs. Mediumship can show the way by the realisation that we are all unified by our inner spirit.

THE GRACE OF PRAYER

Prayer has immeasurable value, as true prayer enlarges the soul, when we pray with sincerity and love it has the capacity to change space and bring about a transformation. If you have ever visited a holy place or temple where for many years people have met together in an atmosphere of love and devotion, the prayers live in the ether and can be felt as tangible energy that touches the deepest self. Prayer enriches the soul and is the art of presence. What would be the prayer of your soul? Allow yourself to contemplate this statement and let the answer arise from deep within you, maybe the memory of why you are here upon the earth will awaken as a gentle knowing and it will serve to be a reminder to you in the days to come and help facilitate an alignment with your soul's purpose.

If it is true, as is commonly believed, then you can't have a thought without it affecting the whole universe. To cultivate an inner state of prayer creates a sense of the sacred in the ordinary and how can anything created ever be ordinary.

In the words of the poet, Francis Thompson (1859-1907):

All things by immortal power,

Near or far.

Hiddenly,

To each other linked are,

That thou canst not stir a flower

Without troubling of a star.

Think of the abundance of benefits that can arise for someone who lives a life from a state of real prayer. When each act, no matter how mundane, is performed with a sense of connection, life can become a living prayer and even though it may be hard to fulfil, small effort amounts to great effort when made with good intent. It doesn't matter that we try, yet sometimes fail, it only matters that at the end of the day we have genuinely made an effort.

As we move through life, we all encounter times when life calls us to forgive. Forgiveness has nothing to do with religion but is instead a choice we make, to both grow and let go, by doing so we contribute to freeing ourselves from the chains created by the past and give ourselves permission to live in the present moment. When one person forgives, two people have the potential to be healed. Everyone has a need to forgive and at times be forgiven, there is not one person alive who has lived such a virtuous life that they have nothing to be forgiven. We all make mistakes; we are only human after all. The secret is not to get hung up on the mistakes but view each from the perspective of the lesson to be learned. When someone we know or love causes us suffering, it's very easy for the hurt to overshadow all their other good qualities, so try not to allow your mind to dwell on the pain. It is easy to say the words 'I forgive', but words can be empty. For forgiveness to be real it must flow not from the head but from the heart, where it enters through the door of feeling, only when we can engage with feeling does it become authentic. To forgive another is transformative and becomes prayer in action; it is the gift we give ourselves.

Our own self is the temple of God and prayer is the alter, if you feel inspired to go to a church of a particular kind it should be to share God, not to find God. How can you find God? God can only be experienced through each one of us by a process of realisation and recognition.

Have you ever looked, I mean really looked, into the heart of a flower to see its delicate feather-like veins? There lies a sophisticated universe of wonder, an exquisite world perfectly formed. Whatever is within the essence of the flower exists within us. Petal upon petal of God unfolding. Within each is God's signature, our own unique essence of the divine.

The mystic and poet William Blake conveyed a knowledge that comes from a deep-seated understanding of the universality of all life, recognising that, essentially, we all belong one to the other, saying "I am in you and you are in me, mutual in divine love".

It is not enough to use words when we pray for prayer to be real, it must flow from a deep well of love within us, because of this no-one can teach another to pray - it is a state of soul remembering, of grace. The authenticity of prayer is our capacity to be at one with the essence of the words; by doing this we give life to, and invite, the prayer into being as a living reality, just as music has a vitality of its own and can be likened to a state of soul, our prayer should be a reflection of our divine nature, merging as a deep harmony with all that is within us and a recognition this life and moment is sacred. It is important to ask ourselves what within us actually prays?

If considering cultivating mediumistic powers of awareness I would, without doubt, encourage a deep effort to learn the art of real prayer as it leads the way and imbues the person who prays with spiritual power. In a world where an inherent sacred power is becoming manufactured and mediumship is classed as nothing more than entertainment, we need to remember the sacred if only in our hearts.

When you pray for another, it has an ability to enrich both the person who prays and the one who receives. There is something almost magical about being held in the prayers of another; it is as though an invisible power surrounds us and we are bathed within the silent embrace of love. The impact and power of this energy and the difference prayer may make within our lives is immeasurable.

EMERGING SENSITIVITY

A word on sensitivity, as it can come in waves as our mediumistic nature begins to be awakened. Sensitivity can also lead to experiencing a stirring of all the emotional responses which may have been felt, but suppressed, throughout our life. So often we move into survival mode when encountering loss of some kind and fail to honour the deeper, more real, emotions that lie silently beneath the surface waiting for an invitation to emerge. Additionally, you may also encounter being more affected by the suffering of others as the Zen monk, Ryokan (1758-1831) so beautifully states:

O that my monks robe,

Were wide enough

To gather up all the suffering people

In this floating world.

I can only suggest that you honour these new-found sensitivities and that you allow each one to reveal its story and meaning in fullness. Dive deep into the bottomless ocean of feeling to discover a pearl. For in the process of acknowledging there awaits a treasure that will enable you to identify with the diverse range of human experience, of both those still living their earthly life and those in the spirit world, who will communicate through you. The spirit communicators are resourceful beyond measure and will draw upon every gem of experience and emotional state you have ever encountered.

30

Sensitivity can be said to be both a blessing and a burden as you feel things more deeply than most. The blessing far outweighs anything negative and you learn over time to acknowledge but not to over-indulge. Sensitivity should always be expressed as activity, by reaching out to others, for if you are going to be any use helping people through loss or suffering you have to learn the skillful balance of understanding in a supportive manner, but not allow yourself to be so affected by the pains of another that you can no longer be the clear channel for the spirit world.

There exists a polarity in sensitivity as it can both separate and unite at the same time. When we meet some people, it is clear that we share a commonality of purpose and have a mutual love and respect, whereas with others a gulf or divide can emerge as it becomes apparent their thought processes differ vastly from our own. It is always best to seek to be in the presence of those you feel at home with when spiritual powers begin to awaken. "The secret, Alice, is to surround yourself with people that make your heart smile, it's only then that you'll find wonderland" (Lewis Carroll) - I find this an interesting quote, when you ponder on its meaning and how wonderland can be translated as an eternal peace within. To learn to be in the world but not of the world is sometimes necessary to simply live

When the burden of life overwhelms you, I suggest you read a book on the life of one of the many great spiritual teachers of our time, of course it won't change your problems, but you may just find the capacity to draw upon a little of the power that radiated from these remarkable souls. You can't help but be inspired when you read of the adversities that have been overcome and challenges conquered, in the history of the human spirit. Look at Nelson Mandela, when after 21 long years in captivity in the harshest of conditions, he was offered his freedom he replied, "I cannot and will not give any undertaking at a time when I and you, the people are not free", he said "Your freedom and mine cannot be separated". In the ordinary lives of many people behind a real or a self-created door, there is often great suffering. If you look a little closer and use your sensitivity you just may see it. What is this invisible power that inspires people to acts of greatness, where courage and justice flow like a mighty river to nourish the souls of others? It is the same power that is the very essence of us all and is the reason why the seed of a pine tree can remember the trees of 20 million years ago. As the old saying goes, the best way to forget yourself is to lose yourself in the service of others. We can never hope to change the world; this too great a task, but what we can do is be a positive force for good in the lives of those around us and that always includes, without exception, showing acceptance and loving kindness to oneself.

Kindness has a powerful ripple effect, one small drop of kindness can create ripples of limitless love. As human beings I believe we are wired to be kind, after all we are told that being benevolent releases happy endorphins in the brain and is even responsible for more happy chemicals than eating lots of chocolate, which creates serotonin. Unlike chocolate, where the intake should be in moderation, acts of kindness need have no limit. In fact, the more compassion you show every day the greater your life expectancy, according to the latest research. Sensitivity and kindness belong to each other, like sunshine and rain, in a world where people now more than ever have a hunger to be loved and understood.

To develop mediumship is not enough, as human and spiritual beings we should develop the power of our own spirit.

EXERCISE

Try sitting quietly and allow your attention to move within, bring a deep sense of connection to awareness of the breath and being home to yourself within the body, within the moment. Gently allow yourself to observe the rise and fall of the breath, creating a sense of peace.

When an inner stillness has been achieved, and the mind is no longer distracted ask yourself.

What do I really believe is true?

What is my commitment, to a natural process of inner development?

What do I mean by god?

What is my offering I give to life?

Further reading:

How to Know Higher Worlds, Rudolf Steiner, Steiner Books

CHAPTER TWO.

THE MEDITATIVE MIND

Put your thoughts to sleep

do not let them cast a shadow

over the moon of your heart.

Let go of thinking. Rumi

Meditation is an important aspect of spiritual growth but is also contributory to the unfolding of mediumship itself. The meditative mind encourages enhanced well-being, a deep connection and realisation of our true nature. If practised daily it can bring about an inner transformation, it is not an end, but facilitates inward progression and has positive effects on every level of our being, physically, mentally, emotionally and spiritually.

There exists as many methods of approach as there are days in the year. It is really by practice that we discover which method is best suited to our needs. Collective studies have found that regular meditators experience an integration of both right and left hemispheres of the brain, which enhances concentration, can heighten creativity and promotes a feeling of wellbeing. This can ultimately lead to what the mystics called 'the gateway to oneness' and deepens a sense of interconnection with all life, a feeling very often experienced by the spirituality awakened within every religion; spirituality is the art of homecoming, where we truly come home to ourselves and acknowledge our unity of spirit.

When you first begin to practise meditation it soon becomes apparent that it is no effortless process, to remain centred can take many years of practice. During the early stages, thoughts can jump from one thing to another and frequently, as if from nowhere, experiences we thought had long been forgotten can rise to the surface. Initially both time and practice are required and the need to persist long enough to enable the mind to become settled each time you attempt to meditate; be aware the first ten minutes are often spent getting behind the distractions of the mind. To learn how to allow the thought processes to gently dissolve promotes stillness and helps to cultivate a willingness to be fully present. Once there is nowhere else for the mind to go thought finds its rest in silence, stillness of the body and calming of the restless wave of thought, free of mental effort to actively achieve this or that, beyond the desire to see images or perceive, just to be. Developing the routine of sitting every day will bring its own reward.

When we meditate, we take refuge from the stress and strain of our modern lives. Our ancestors had their own stresses fighting off predators and hunting for food, but the stress that faces each one of us in our modern lives could be thought equal to that of our ancestors, dealing as we must with the many challenges of our current times. This coupled with our highly sensitive nervous systems and the refining of our spiritual awareness means now more than ever before we need to learn just to be still, to be in touch with our own selves and enjoy the refuge in that. "Be still, be still and know that

I am God" (Psalm 46:10) generates a whole new necessity and meaning. If you allow yourself to contemplate this one statement a deeper comprehension will awaken within you, try it and see what doors it may open within.

By learning the art of refraining from investing attention and energy in the past, by not allowing the mind to dwell on the emotional responses that have shaped our lives and our characters and by learning to be truly present in the now, we give ourselves the greatest gift of freedom and maximise our power to take charge of our life and refrain from recreating old behavioural patterns which so frequently keep us trapped in a cycle. As we persist in the resistance of these patterns, we begin to learn from these lessons and to take control of our thoughts and cultivate a beautiful mind.

Just as when we desire to become physically fit, we create a routine and exercise, we need to work out in the gym of our minds and build mental muscle, beginning gently. There is a quiet rhythm that emerges when we learn the art of being completely alive in each moment and the grace of the universe begins to flow through our being, when we are present in ourselves.

The practice of concentration, meditation or the art of mindfulness deepens our perception and by focusing on a word such as love, a mantra, or a sacred passage we help to integrate all our mental energy into a harmonious flow. It is believed that Buddha realised how our minds shape our reality when he stated 'we become what we think about all day long' or to use a more present phrase, energy follows thought and thought attracts its own kind. This is an opinion commonly shared by many. Surely then if we concentrate on love and loving, eventually our whole being will respond even on a cellular level encouraging greater harmony. This type of practice I believe is a stepping-stone to greater growth and awareness, is one which enhances and quickens the power within and ultimately leads to the very heart of true meditative experience.

A beneficial exercise is to just sit peacefully and begin to witness the breath, be in the presence of awareness. Pay attention to the stream of thought-flow which arises, but do not allow yourself to become distracted, instead like the autumn leaves as they gently fall and find a place of rest, allow the mental activity to become inactivity, without intense striving, refrain from any need to coerce or manipulate the mind but rest gently and gracefully in the presence of awareness itself. Be aware of being aware and dwell in your innermost centre where your sense of perception arises. Begin to realise you are part of all life and all life is part of you, all creation both seen and unseen as integral, ultimately acknowledging pure awareness as your authentic self. Realise that the universe is your garden and everything within it exists because of you and your capacity to perceive it.

The Buddhists have a quirky saying when beginning to teach people how to meditate, "you should sit in meditation for at least twenty minutes a day, unless you are too busy, then you should sit for an hour".

The practice of meditation can be likened to the energy of a tree in winter when it is withdrawn from the surface and drawn back into the roots. As practice deepens it is very similar to that of the tree with all focus and attention moving within, to seek nourishment from the roots of the spirit.

As in the famous painting in St Paul's Cathedral, 'The light of the world' by William Holman Hunt, of Jesus holding a light at the entrance to a door which has no handles on the outside for it must be opened from within, no one can open the door for us on our inner journey, we must do it ourselves. However, the very act of so doing invites an awareness of our infinite self and all the illusions which have held us back from self-discovery fall away. It is a symbolic process in a language which surpasses all religious and cultural differences, that conveys the need to learn the art of mental stillness, of inner peace, by creating a sacred space in the temple of self, so we can truly hear and truly see beyond our sensory perception.

If we are diligent in our efforts, dormant powers will begin to awaken, abilities we never knew we possessed will seek expression. The world around us may still be the same, but our deepened perception will mean we view things differently. The mundane is transformed to the divine, the ordinary to the extraordinary.

METTA BHAVANA

Metta is a Pali word which essentially means loving kindness, bhavana implies cultivation. So, when we practise 'metta bhavana' we promote cultivation of loving kindness towards ourself and others. It is not enough to dwell in this state of mind whilst meditating but should be developed within our own heart, our own being, in the daily living of our lives, for this is where the real practice begins and ends in genuine effort. Especially when we find ourselves in challenging situations, when life calls us to listen to the voice of reason and compassion rather than intolerance and anger. Through connection with our self, we become open to have connection with others.

SETTING THE INTENT

The first steps towards metta begin with setting the intent. Whilst meditating, the mind is more open and receptive to suggestion. This is beneficial particularly when making a conscious effort to embody loving kindness and to wish peace and fulfilment to all, as a part of the practice. Because of past conditioning and hurt many of us find it difficult to trust ourselves enough to love completely, as loving is often associated with pain but any effort to undo the tangled knots of our lives will enhance our whole life, which will benefit not only ourselves but everyone we meet on the road of existence. Of course, loving requires each of us to be vulnerable, but if we can risk the invitation to love unconditionally, we experience the world and everyone in it through the eyes anew. After all, life requires that we are kind to each other and to acknowledge that everyone has their own pain despite often being hidden, layer upon layer. It is important to remember that we will never see someone else's experience. Very often people hide their suffering behind a smile and never allow their inner world to be expressed. Loving acceptance creates the possibility of a better world where each person is valued and accepted for who they are.

PREPARATION FOR MEDITATION:

- *Allow yourself to be present to your body, notice your posture and any areas of tension or discomfort you may have been carrying*

- *Take two or three deep breaths making a conscious effort to be present within the experience*

- *Do not allow the mind to dwell on the past or to be preoccupied with the future*

- *Begin to direct the movement of the breath to the heart*

There are many adapted variations of how to achieve metta, but in all there are four basic stages:

Stage 1: Loving Kindness to Our Own Self

Imagine the heart is like the sun, which by outwards refraction radiates and shines upon all life, become as the sun and shine the light of inner radiance. This loving power illuminates your mind and your entire being including your physical body.

Now feel the warmth and power of the sun of love moving through your entire being and realise that to truly love another we must begin with the first step, to learn to love ourselves, the fruit of love is forgiveness, the blossoms of which are petals of freedom and deepening compassion.

Stage 2: Loving Kindness to Others

It is important to extend loving kindness to others especially those we have shared the journey of life with, our family and friends. Imagine these people to be held within the warmth of the light of the sun of loving kindness and feel this love flowing from you unconditionally. See those you are connected to as radiant and happy.

Stage 3: Learning to Love Altruistically

This next stage is more challenging as the practice of loving kindness requires us to learn to love altruistically, we need to embrace in our awareness even those who have been the cause of our suffering. Do not discriminate who you will radiate your love upon and hold in your focus; all those you thought you had long forgotten, they need your love and to be free from the burden of past mistakes.

There is not one person alive who is completely free from ever having made a mistake, it is of course part of the human experience and condition. But everyone has a choice to learn from the past, so the same mistakes are not made in the future, allowing the grace of forgiveness to take root in our soul will facilitate spiritual growth.

Stage 4: Learning to Love All Humanity

Lastly turn your awareness to include those you have never met, all humanity. For all belong to the same family of man and share the capacity to love and to show kindness.

May I be happy and free from suffering.

May I be at peace.

May all beings be happy and free from suffering.

May all beings be at peace.

In the art of extending our capacity to love we are transformed inwardly. If during the practice certain memories rise to the surface of your mind it could be indicative of a need to acknowledge an unhealed wound and to use this moment to be the catalyst for change. By allowing true authenticity, and the ability to identify and embrace these deep-rooted feelings together with gentle effort, you will find progress will be made. Eventually it becomes easier and the results are a treasure of which there is no earthly comparison. It is not enough to cultivate the unfolding of spiritual powers if we haven't first made effort to work on our inner self and look at our true reflection in the mirror of awareness.

Mediumistic powers and abilities shall be left behind us when we pass, but any effort made to spiritualise ourselves will be carried with us through eternity. It is essential to ask the question, do we like the company we keep when alone? Can we face our own self in the space which exists when we are on our own, or are we inclined to fill the silence with activity? There is no room for two on the road to self-inquiry and self-acceptance, we must take this journey alone, but the results are immeasurable.

To incorporate a spiritual practice into the living of our daily lives is vital, how can we truly help another if first we haven't helped our own self? By the act of understanding the complexities of emotions and reactions that govern our response to situations we find ourselves in, we come become better human and spiritual beings and the expression of mediumistic powers will be understood by measure of truly embodying the ability to be of help to another.

The benefits of practising metta are their own reward. To meditate daily on universal love means the acquisition of inner power; the grace of this has the potential not only to heal but additionally to bring about a deep transformation. To heal and free your own self has an impact on others, the blessing of practising compassion softens our heart and creates the space to experience freedom of the heart and enables each of us to return to who we really are.

MANTRA AS A TOOL FOR GROWTH

The practice of using a mantra can be very beneficial. It is not, as some people believe, the same as using a positive affirmation. There is a great deal more power within a mantra which potentially has the ability to disempower the rational mind, freeing the person who chants from the crystallised pattern of limiting behaviours that is often embedded in the subconscious mind.

All mantra creates a vibration in the body which can have intense physical benefits. It is believed these vibrations produce powerful neuro linguistic effects, which induce a sense of inner calm and well-being. A mantra can help by gently diffusing stress, the rhythm encourages a flow of energy which can be conducive in regulating the chemicals in the brain by releasing endorphins and stopping stress hormones from creating damage.

When we repeat the names of God contained within the mantra, the presence of God within each of us is uncovered and the potential to know oneself revealed. It is as though we come home to ourselves in the realisation of our true infinite nature. Regular practice deepens our awareness in a profound way, beyond anything words could begin to describe.

It is traditional to have a personal mantra given to you, but If you haven't got the luxury of a teacher who can recommend a specific mantra, then it is always best to listen to various ones until you feel a deep connection with the sound and vibration by you allowing your intuition or the mantra itself to speak to you.

If you feel drawn to use a mantra as part of your spiritual practice it is important you remember the value created by repetition as it should always be recited from a place of deep motivation and awareness, bringing the totality of your attention to blend with the experience. This will ultimately help the mantra to help you and therefore to work its magic. It is the gateway to other states of consciousness. If we develop a disciplined routine, we will find in our heart what words such as love and bliss really mean. Practising a mantra enables the soul to remember and rediscover the peace which was our original nature before our material life got in the way!

Try when working with your chosen mantra to find a connection between the movement of the mantra and the breath, by allowing yourself to be fully present. After years of practice, it's as if the mantra not only becomes an integrated part of you, but you will find it's as though the mantra remembers you and has a life force of its own. I say this because there have been times in my life when I have been under extreme stress and without even consciously reciting my mantra it has begun to move through my mind, almost encouraging a different flow of thought into a more harmonious direction.

We can hear about mantras from people who use them and read about the power contained within the practice and I strongly believe, like a lot of things in life, that our own mantra will find us when the time is right.

EXPERIMENT

Explore, the suggested exercise and see if it works for you?

First, make sure you are sitting in a comfortable position, consciously direct your attention to your body and begin to feel relaxed. Next, gently observe the breath, just being aware of the rise and fall of your own natural rhythm of breathing. Now allow a number, from one to six to arise in your awareness, without searching simply let this happen on its own. You may see the number in your mind's eye, or even sense, or hear it, no one way is any better than the other, everyone is different!

Next, look up the number and the mantra associated; you have sub-consciously selected. Does the meaning resonate or does it just feel right, maybe the mantra chose you? If you feel yourself to be in harmony with the mantra, dedicate time each day to practise. Try reciting it, until a rhythm begins to move through you, and its beneficial power encourages the qualities, your chosen mantra embodies.

1. **AUM or OM:** Is considered to be the most commonly used mantra of all. It is classed, as the primordial sound of the universe, as within the sound all other sounds emerge and is the reason why, it is often referred to as the cosmic hymn of the universe. Om is believed to illuminate the mind and encourages an innate connection with each other, the recognition that we all possess the same divine origin.

2. **SITA RAM:** Promotes a deep sense of truth (Ram) and the soul of virtue (Sita) helps balance both sides of the brain. it is believed to improve health by removing negativity and impurities from body and mind.

3. **AHAM PREMA:** This mantra is pronounced, Aah-ham-pree-mah. Its

meaning is powerful and translates as 'I am divine love'. This is a simply beautiful mantra, encompassing the ability to not only align with, but embody divine love as a living reality.

4. **OM NAMAH SHIVAYA:** Means attainment of self-realisation and helps facilitate dissolving of the ego. The nature of the mantra is calling upon the spiritual self, in the seeking of truth and is an invitation to know your true nature. it is also to thought to represent all the elements, earth, water, fire, air, and ether.

5. **HAM SAH:** Unlike most of the other Hindu and Buddhist mantras, derives from Hebrew and is an embodiment of the powerful statement, 'I am that I am' in recognition of the conscious presence of God in all life, both within and without.

6. **OM TARA:** Originates from the Tibetan Buddhist tradition and is believed to be the purest representation of the Buddha, and reflects a deep realisation that the world of form, the play of our lives is purely a manifestation of divine power. Yet it is necessary to look with awareness beyond the impermanent to the real. Tara, means star and is guiding us to the other shore, ultimate reality.

MEDITATIVE SELF HEALING

We humans are by nature uncomfortable when asking for something for our own selves, but it is imperative that we try to put our own house in order before venturing out and trying to heal the world! Those who freely give to others often have a tendency to give their whole self away without leaving much in the cup of remembrance of their own needs. So, the following practice can help by spending a little time and effort nurturing yourself.

Make sure you are sitting somewhere quiet where you will not be disturbed.

Ensure you are sitting comfortably. Move your attention to the breath, and for a few moments observe the unique rhythm the breath makes. Now move your attention up your body starting from your feet and working upwards towards the head. Listen to your body intently; you may not be aware of anything at first but after your thoughts settle you may find the intelligence of the body begins to speak to you, it may be gentle at first as a soft knowing. Are there any areas that draw your attention? If so, listen more deeply, possibly a colour will arise and if it does the colour will be a messenger conveying a story. Again, invoke the quality of truly listening until you begin to hear, every single cell within our body has a consciousness of its own - a divine intelligence.

Once you have located any areas of disharmony within the body, invite harmony and healing to this area. It may help by visualising a light and focusing on the feeling of wholeness and health. It is important to come to the realisation that the healing is already taking place, not in the distant future as a vague hope but in this given moment. This is vitally important as the universe only understands the energetic statement you are making right here and now, this is all that is real.

In identifying a health problem it is easy for a person to become 'the problem' until the condition is all that is experienced; the self becomes forgotten and buried behind the illness. I recall a dear friend who was a spiritual healer who I had the privilege to know, on being diagnosed with cancer told me with an air of positivity in her voice "I have cancer, but cancer hasn't got me". Needless to say she lived to conquer the disease and eventually passed as all of us must but from old age, or should I say the spirit outgrowing the need for a body!

The person who feels secure in his or her own self never feels threatened by the achievements of another, it is only possible to feel secure in yourself if you have made an effort to first heal yourself. To know is the path to under-standing and the liberator from fear, it helps with the realisation that each person is bringing a unique quality to existence and then we can celebrate in another's success!

We all have to drink deeply from our own cup and discover our own inner treasures in order to survive the living of life. We can do this by cultivating an openness of heart and mind and refraining from a need to judge ourselves or others, as in the end we realise as the spiritual guru Ramana did. When asked by a devotee "how do we deal with others?", he replied "there are no others". Profound words indeed from an awakened spiritual teacher, yet if you look deeply enough all spiritual and religious traditions are pointing in the same direction.

SITTING IN THE POWER VERSUS MEDITATION?

A lot of people get extremely confused regarding the difference between sitting in the power and actual meditative practice. Is there a difference and which method is most beneficial? The answer is yes there is a difference, but one way is not necessarily better than the other. It largely depends upon your aims and intention, but why not do both? In short, meditation is about going within to encourage a deeper comprehension of self, whilst sitting in the power can be described as merging in a state of oneness with the very essence of life.

Each day dedicate a short while to your preferred meditative practice. Additionally, if you intend exploring the developing of your mediumistic awareness, it is helpful also to allow yourself to be passive and invite the presence of those in the spirit world to draw close, not to actively engage in communicating rather, just to rest sustained within the power and presence of the spirit. This facilitates an expansion in our mind and consciousness and awakens the realisation that you are a part of all life and all life is a part of you.

I believe that sitting in the power will nourish your own spiritual strength, which those in the spirit world can draw upon when you work with your mediumship. I liken it to putting money in a savings account but instead of money you are banking or storing spiritual power which will sustain you when actively needed. Just as the earth nourishes all forms of life, the power will encourage the blossoming of spiritual abilities.

How can power be defined? It's like saying 'how is love to be defined?'; surely, it's all relative to the individual, each person describing love will relay a different interpretation. For love can only be felt within, as an inner state of being, therefore be experienced rather than seen. In ancient Sanskrit there are ninety-six words for love, in ancient Persian eighty, in Greek three and in English only one. It makes the English language seem a little impoverished and our comprehension of the many expressions of love limited.

The power then is the very essence of love itself, the life force of the universe, and when we allow ourselves to be at one with it those in the spirit world become a conscious part of our awareness. In the deepest silence we develop our sensitivity and begin to hear the inner sounds contained within all life. How we can even begin to perceive other realms of existence if we have not first attuned ourselves to all that speaks to us here, for the earth and life itself is filled with the grandeur of God.

Breath is the unifying power which connects life to consciousness and our physical body to our thoughts, breath is the bridge and by calming our breathing a natural calming of the mind will follow.

First it is essential to acknowledge the power within you, as both infinite and divine. By a process of recognition, it becomes possible to express this in and through our spiritual awareness, beyond the boundaries and limitations so often created by mind, body awareness. It is not enough to believe, belief alone is not sufficient. The power of God within requires each of us to know. Only then can a real process of transformation take place enabling spiritual potential to be fully expressed.

Of all the people we visit we need to visit ourselves the most! When we can learn the art of being still and silent, it brings about a capacity to be more in harmony with the rhythm of our life and more at peace with our own self.

Each time we meet someone for the first time we have an opportunity we are not normally aware of. How we engage in the experience of 'seeing' the person is very often either fear or love based. Practising meditation can encourage the start of seeking ways to recognise we are an intrinsic and vital part of the whole. Try, when you meet someone, to look through the eyes of the spirit and not the ego and you will have the capacity to dissolve and break down walls; inwardly affirming to truly see another from this perspective means we see through the eyes of awareness. We can then respond with an openness of heart which has the capacity to heal the unspoken wound and embrace another silently in the language of love.

EXERCISE:

- *Try meditating – as you do so try to disassociate from your physical body for a while and simply ask yourself, "Who am I? " Can you remember who you were, before the world told you, who you should be and you became so conditioned as to forget.*

- *Remember you are not the sum totality of your physical self, or even your circumstances the real you cannot be limited to the locality of your physical form or the span of a lifetime.*

- *Imagine hanging up all the labels you have identified with by putting them all on a coat rack. Visualise each role as a coloured garment. Then see what remains once you have removed all the outer layers. Notice how you feel, do you feel a sense of relief? Or maybe freedom? from now on try to be more aware of the real you and not the person that others have labelled or perceived you to be. To learn the value of the realisation that beyond all the attachments to these conditions you are the ever-present light of awareness.*

CHAPTER THREE

OUR INFINITE SELF

"*How fortunate are you and I,*

Whose home is timelessness,

We who have wondered down

From fragrant mountains of eternal now

To frolic in such mysteries as birth and death

A day (or maybe even less)"

E.E. Cumminings

We participate in the rhythmic dance of life and our physical body is nothing more than a piece of clothing which we wear for the duration of our earthly life, just as we are not the cars we drive. Without the driver at the wheel the car would remain stationary and would be nothing more than just an empty shell. The secret is not to get caught in the trap of thinking, which makes you believe the body is the real you.

The question arises then, 'if I am not the body who is this self who perceives, animates the physical form and has conscious awareness, who loves, thinks and dreams?' Those who have an understanding of spiritual truths will undoubtably declare, of course, you are that which is timeless and eternal, the spirit. One day all who have touched the earth with their presence will pass, silently through the looking glass.

There exists little consensus on what consciousness actually is. Nearly all inquiry up to the present time that has emerged in the field of trying to fathom an understanding of the nature of consciousness has done little more than study brain activity and unfortunately has failed to reveal any in-depth insight regarding the nature of consciousness. For the entire experience of consciousness is subjective. Consciousness is still one of the perplexing mysteries which exists, as it cannot be quantified and by its very nature is elusive, just like an autumn mist moving silently across the landscape only to disappear eludes the observer. Only the spiritual gurus and teachers, by direct experience and understanding, have described this most intangible state. Only consciousness can know the nature of consciousness; just like awareness - we do not have awareness, we are awareness.

Likewise, research into near-death and out-of-body experiences becomes by its very nature somewhat inconclusive and subjective. After all it is necessary for someone to temporarily die first for the research to take place, then once resuscitated have a lucid recollection of proceedings that need to be based on information which can be substantiated. Yet despite all the obstacles involved there have been some extremely thought-provoking results over the years of inquiry and some most remarkable stories have emerged.

Pioneering spiritual science is arriving at the possibility that the brain may be the receiver of consciousness rather than the creator of it. This is a step closer to the realisation that our true nature is pure consciousness.

Collective studies over many years of people who have had near-death experiences share a commonality in many aspects.

- Nearly all people experienced a change in their thought processes.

- Their thinking became quicker and each person encountered a noticeable difference in their emotional state.

- A sensation of being immersed in light which led to a feeling of euphoria.

- Deep feelings of peace and love overwhelmed them.

- A strange lack of interest in their material life occurred and all that had given them concern whilst in the physical form no longer appeared relevant.

- Nearly all had visions of the future and a realisation where past, present and future appeared to be one.

- Many frequently met those known to them who had previously died, but were told it wasn't their time and to go back.

- In some cases, they have met with people most recently passed, even before other relatives have known this to have actually happened, proving it wasn't some illusory projection of the mind

Comparing this to the descriptions of the mystics and visionaries of the past it is apparent that great parallels exist. A process of perceiving the world no longer through the narrow lens of fragmentation but from the perspective of wholeness occurs, together with a feeling of euphoria. On being freed from the limitations of the body one becomes in touch with the infinite self; having had a near-death experience, life can never be the same again. One could argue that this logically justifies why it is frequently reported by those who, having had an NDE, have an innate desire to live their life very differently from before. If we begin to express unity in our lives, we not only help ourselves but everyone else, even those we have never met.

According to many eastern religious traditions all suffering occurs because we lose our sense of self and view life from the limited perspective of separation, rather than wholeness. The sacred journey comes back to this one realisation, we all originate from the same source, and despite being fooled in our thinking, in truth we have never really left that place.

As the outer world reflects our inner life, attuning to the still small voice of the spirit, we create the way for inter-spirituality. The kind of spirituality which transcends the barrier of cultural and religious differences. Inter-spirituality can be the nucleus that binds all together in the recognition that we are one and respects and realises the beauty in all.

The power we call God expresses itself in each life differently, everyone is born with the vibratory signature of their own level of consciousness. When someone is born upon the earth and draws their first breath an exchange of energy with the universe occurs, it is said that a light flashes across the heavens and the sound of the soul is heard throughout all creation.

We incarnate at the level at which the spirit is in harmony with the mind and come equipped with all the qualities necessary for the journey ahead. A new chapter in the book of life is being written, a page being turned, another body of expression; but not a new life for the soul has always existed in other realities, far beyond all that the physical senses can comprehend. For birth and death are just a parenthesis in eternity.

We agree to take specific learning agenda in each life according to the measure of what we need to learn, which will help facilitate a deep enrichment of the soul and create an opportunity for growth. The goal is surely to achieve the highest level of humanity and spirituality possible. By doing so we will each add a new dimension and colour to existence.

The physical reality in which we live is a world of appearances and is also a mirror of spirit realms. The spirit world is the world of cause, the physical level is the world of effect. For everything that appears will one day disappear, yet this is not true of the spirit. This material reality is a relative world of time and space, where duality and difference exist, this gives birth to creative expression. The material world requires the creative pressure, brought about by opposites, just as a diamond is formed deep down within the heart of the earth by intense heat followed by cold and pressure, the metaphor of the diamond and the ability to clearly refract the light represents the soul and our potential to reflect the light of our inner being, even through the trials of human existence and the delusions of the small self.

Although our world is essentially a realm of duality, it is also an enormous trick of the senses and our perception. We look up at the heavens at the brightest of stars in wondrous formations. Stars whose light years take so long to reach us that they no longer exist. Planet earth, our home, is suspended in space, rotating on its axis held there by gravitational forces all of which are invisible to the human eye. It is considered verifiable that matter is frozen light, not in some esoteric sense but in real terms. "For every particle of light that constitutes matter, there are also a billion particles of light that are not matter. This essentially means matter, despite our taking everything in the physical world so very often for granted, is considerably rare! Even the oxygen we breathe is the recycled air which was around in the days of Jesus and Buddha". Matthew Fox

The whole of space is alive could we but see and nothing is as it would appear to the limited capacity of our five senses which, I may add, are but a tiny lens to filter the wonders of creation through. Within the space in the room in which you are now sitting there exists more energy and information than the entire material universe; however, all this energy and information do not interfere with one another as they do not occupy the same point in space and time. In the trance teachings one of my spirit inspirers once said, "here within this room, there are worlds within worlds, breathtakingly beautiful landscapes, rolling fields and meadows of colours beyond anything which can be imagined, where those some have thought dead still exist, could you but see." A concept a little hard to conceive if you have been brought up in a world that would have you believe only in the reality of our physical senses, but if you can stretch your thinking a little and consider the possibility of an alternative, the world becomes an extraordinary miracle full of wonder.

The spirit world, invisible to normal vision, touches spiritual vision. The concept that some religious traditions have, believing that it is wrong to wake up the so-called 'dead' and that communication is the work of the devil, could not be farther from the truth. Try entering into a conversation with those who have made their transition and you will realise they are more alive than most of us left behind who are burdened with the trials of 'life'. This age-old belief has suppressed man's inherent ability for centuries and has affected the collective unconscious. It arises from around 425 A.D when Constantinople, at the council of Nicaea and from the fear of losing power, introduced new laws to discourage people from communicating with the spirit of the dead and communing with higher powers, making any efforts to communicate punishable by death, a deterrent indeed! Now we live in an age when mankind is finally waking up to the realisation of his eternal self and the natural powers of his own spirit. As Walt Whitman so aptly expressed "There will soon be no more priests. Their work is done, everyman shall be his own priest"

You could say then everything that exists which is material will one day cease to be. Only the eternal things such as spirit will remain; doesn't that sound a touch familiar? Surely this is what one of the followers of Jesus was referring to in the gospel of St Paul, 'So we fix our eyes not on what is seen, but on what is unseen, since what is seen is temporary, but what is unseen is eternal' 2 Corinthians, 4.18. The world is catching up now, just a mere two and a half thousand years later, aren't we all just a little slow. Or has the world of the senses been such a distraction we have got well and truly waylaid, but better late than never.

As the Sufi mystic Rumi stated,

"Oh my God, our intoxicated eyes have blurred our vision.

Our burdens have become heavy forgive us.

You are hidden, and yet from east to west, you have filled the world

with your radiance.

Your light is more magnificent than sunrise or sunset and you are the

innermost consciousness revealing the secrets we hold"

.

Gently the wise mystics showed the way to truth like a finger pointing to the stars, the light of which brightens the path before us even when it is obscured by the shadows cast by the doubts of our rational mind.

Nothing is as it would first seem, Albert Einstein, who said "matter is merely an illusion, albeit a very persistent one", was truly not only an amazing theoretical physicist but also a visionary. This brings us to the greatest of illusions - time. It would of course be helpful to have Albert Einstein himself here at this point then maybe he could 'cast some light upon the matter', for Einstein's discoveries paved the way for an entirely new understanding of our relationship with space and time. His concept of time intriguingly supports what the mystics have revealed; that when experiencing a heightened sense of awareness, the past the present and the future co-exist within the same moment and are illusions we project on the seamless garment of time. How often have spiritual mediums, working within the power and presence of the spirit, foretold of events yet to come. For it is the relationship that one thing has to another within this state that has relevance and meaning. In this heightened awareness everything exists within the same breath of a moment.

Einstein was as much a mystic as he was a theoretical physicist, just don't tell anyone from the world of science that as you may not like their reply. In fact, Einstein had such a curious nature as to the very mysteries of the universe that he arranged to meet at his home in the outskirts of Berlin the Bengali poet laureate, mystic, philosopher and musician Rabindranath Tagore, to discuss the most fundamental questions of human existence. Two brilliant minds conversing in a dance of possibility, the cosmic questions of human existence, the nature of reality and consciousness. How I wish I could have been present at that meeting to bear witness to the birth of such an incredible meeting of hearts and minds. How the world needs these free thinkers that dare to tread the unknown path.

Our spiritual self does not belong in a world which is bound by time, that is why when spirit loved ones communicate with us, they can do so in a natural way as theirs is a journey in love and not distance.

Intriguingly time, then, is not only relative but is a perception of the mind. If we place our consciousness in the past, the past comes alive, project our awareness to the future and the future is born. Time, it can be said, is purely man-made and has no reality except in our own inner mental concepts. An energetic exchange we have made with the universe. For within each moment there exists everything that has gone before and therefore creates the potential of all that is yet is come. All that has ever existed resides in each of us right now, we are the sum totality of existence. What then is real, you may ask? Reality is that which when you stop believing in it doesn't go away! Whether you choose to believe in life after death doesn't really matter too much, other than the fact that it enriches the lives of those that do of course. One day, at some time, somewhere, you will find out for certain when you kiss goodbye to your physical body and those who believe and those who choose not to, will meet regardless and sweet the joy will be of lamenting 'I told you so'!

The spirituality-awakened creative souls all knew this; their states of consciousness gave birth to a new-found state of awareness. As life eternally weaves its multi-coloured tapestry, the weaving is in time, although life itself is timeless. The spirit is not in time or space but in eternity. A more accurate description would be to say we are timeless beings. You do not begin or end but purely and simply exist, just as in the natural world, where you do not perceive the division between spring and summer, one flows unseeingly into the other an endless rhythm of life, so it is with our own lives as we progress from dimension to dimension shedding the old, to find ourselves in new levels of reality each one more beautiful than the last.

Our greatest calling or duty to life is to be who we really are, to move beyond the entrapment that other people's expectations may have placed upon us, but how can we possibly be who we are destined to be if we have not stopped long enough to pay attention to this one essential question?

The entire content of our mind is gathered from outside of it, surely what we gather from the outside cannot be a true reflection of what is inside. Are we the originator of our own thoughts or by contrast are we just the receivers of thought, after all our thoughts come and go and clearly do not point the way to the true self. The need arises, then, to question who is this real self? It is possible in our awareness and understanding to consider the deeper implications of this statement and as we do so begin to embrace a larger life, full of possibility and wonder and inwardly move from the conditioned self to the unlimited self.

What have we to fear? Surely it must be only the 'fear of fear itself'. If we transform our thinking and cease to be afraid of death and begin to accept the possibility, what if there is another reality? Then life as we know it may not be all there is.

Communication with those in the world we call unseen is a natural phenom-enon and by its very occurrence cannot be anything other than natural. Just as when those we love have gone for a vacation to another continent, their absence does not mean they cease to exist just because they are out of sight. On reaching their destination it is natural for them to contact loved ones back home, to confirm their safe arrival. Why should it be any different for those who have made the greatest journey mankind can ever take. For, surely, they have an innate desire to relay the truth that life is eternal and to impart the excitement of finding themselves as they were always thinking, feeling and loving.

It is only disbelief clothed in grief that creates a separation, a veil of emotion that forms a divide. Our own selves prevent us from hearing their voice or perceiving their presence. Sometimes a fragment of awareness of their continued presence is captured fleetingly when in a more receptive mood the heart and spirit feel lighter whilst we relive a memory of happier times and, briefly, we touch souls. Love is the most powerful force in the universe and continues just like the light from a distant star that shines on us long after the star has burnt itself out. For life and love are both eternal.

Physical death does not mean the end of a relationship, in fact those who love can experience a deepened sense of being part of each other. By carrying the memory and love within us, it changes who we are and strengthens the love that is shared. How can death destroy that which never dies?

When the time comes to leave our physical self behind, we shall realise that all we can really take into the next life is what we have given away!

If you have ever been in the presence of a friend or family member when passing has been imminent, you may have witnessed a faraway look in the person's eye. It's as though the person you once knew and loved has begun to withdraw their life essence in some way and has fixed their inner gaze on another reality, for their spiritual self has begun the process of becoming most predominate and a fading away of their physical senses has begun to occur. The awareness of other friends and family who have already gone before takes place, as welcomed guests begin to gather round bringing reassurance and awakening the soul-memory of the spirit's true nature and eternal home. We are held silently within the grace and love of those we hold dear, and the burdens and mystery of our physical journey fade away when we cross the threshold of bodily death, when our sacred spirit pass!

A very dear friend of mine who had devoted her entire life to serving the spirit world, as her eyes glazed over in the time leading up to her imminent passing, said with a smile on her face, 'it's so beautiful over there and all those I have loved are here'. In dying we really are born again. It is fear of the unknown which creates a resistance to letting go; if only everyone would realise that which we so often call the unknown is really the known. To return to the source of our being and to embrace our true state of self

63

and make our way home again, how reassuring to know as we draw our last earthly breath that we close our eyes to this world to awaken in another, more beautiful than the last, but as familiar. It is not fiction but fact, just ask those who exist there.

If a tiny baby could think it would be afraid of birth

To leave the only world it had known would seem a kind of death.

But immediately after birth. The child finds itself in the loving arms of

the mother, showered with affection and cared for at every moment.

Passing through death is really a birth into a new and better world.

Those who are left behind should not grieve as if there were no hope.

Life is changed but not taken away. Our dear ones live on,

in a world beautiful beyond anything we could ever imagine.

There they await the day when they will welcome us with joy.

These reassuringly beautiful words are from a 'Roman Catholic Mass card'. Author unknown.

"With an eye made quiet by the power of harmony and the deep power of joy we see into the soul of things". William Wordsworth. In the process of passing, the capacity to see into the soul of things begins to occur and all that once blinded our inner vision becomes known. As the spiritual teacher Ramana was asked by a devoted student when he was close to being released from the burden of his physical body, what will we do without you? He replied but where am I going there is no where to go!

'It is customary to say when someone is passing they are leaving the body, but this is an untrue portrayal, for in reality we are extending the body, death merely liberates us and expands our perception'

Karl Rahner

EXERCISE

THE SPIRIT WORLD

- *Allow yourself to be comfortable making sure you are relaxed. Bring your focus to your physical self and simply notice how your body feels.*

- *Next bring your attention within to the beat of your heart and the soft movement of the breath - observe the quality of each breath.*

- *Now move your awareness to your mind's eye, or the screen of your consciousness. Starting with the present, allow your attention to recall the story of your life, all the events and roles you have played. Remember the joys and the sorrows, people you have met; each has brought a different gift or lesson, yet realising each experience has served to enrich you. Beyond the judgments made by the mind don't identify with any of these experiences, as the dramas of your life unfold before your awareness. Go right back to childhood when you viewed the world through the eyes of innocence and the magic and wonder of existence shone through your eyes, as you perceived the miracle of life.*

- *Now feel the moment you were first born to the world of form and you drew your first breath on your own, no longer dependent upon your mother. Feel the energy of your family, how they had awaited your arrival not knowing who you were going to be yet trusting anyway.*

- *Direct your attention now to being in the safety of the womb the warmth and security which surrounded you in this state of not yet being born.*

- *Now allow your attention to become aware of a soft warm glow of light and just like the beat of the heart this light gently pulsates. It is calling you home, home to the spirit.*

- *Within the light you experience a state of bliss, until within the power all is experienced as divine. Separate as an individual yet one in consciousness - in the same moment all exists. The birth of galaxies and stars, the dance of atoms, the earth and all life forms. The story of creation unravels as the very breath of existence. Just as the drop is part of the ocean yet the ocean is made of each drop the remembrance of being at one awakens.*

- *Now within the remembrance of the spirit's eternal nature you feel the comfort of familiar surroundings and the presence of those you have loved and known are here; they always have been.*

- *This is your eternal home, the true self, the realisation you are just a visitor upon the earth dawns in your awareness. A space which has always existed within you as a memory of heaven. Observe what you feel and see - the shape, form and colours of the landscape. Notice how you have a soul recognition, as those who are your spiritual family draw near. Their shape and form may be different and yet the soul's true perception speaks to you.*

- *Set an intent to recall with clarity all you are experiencing and choose never to forget, and vow to visit the leafy glades of the spirit as being your true reality.*

- *Not all mysteries will be revealed to your awareness, only what is right according to your soul's level of understanding. Yet the more you offer the intent and invite the possibility the more you help it become a reality.*

- *When you have experienced all there is to be revealed to you within this moment, feel yourself being drawn slowly and steadily back to bodily awareness, drifting effortlessly, called back by the recognition there is still more living of your earthly life to be done, but now with the additional knowledge and new-found purpose which has been awakened within you.*

• *Allow the movement of the breath to help you become more present to yourself and feel your awareness and perception through the physical self once more.*

You may ask, 'how do I know it is not just wishful thinking or even imagination?' What is to imagine, for everything that exists first has its origin in thought and surely imagination is the creativity of the soul? Without which nothing would ever have been invented or created. Our world exists because it has its very roots in the foundation built upon by creative spirits who had enough vision to dream and wonder. Does the seed imagine the flower which one day it will become, what secret power is within it that causes it to bloom? Maybe the seed sleeps until the vision of the flower calls to its being to awaken.

Further reading:

The Spiritual Teachings of Ramana Maharshi, Shabhala Classics

CHAPTER FOUR

COLOUR, THE DANCE OF LIGHT

The soul becomes dyed with the colour of its thoughts.

Marcus Aurelius

The mystery of life arises from the play of light. Without light life on planet earth would not have been possible. It is true to say that colours, as Goethe described, are "the children of light"; colour is the bringer of life in all its multiplicity and variety of forms and expression. The human eye is limited by its very nature and has a capacity to perceive within a very small range the visible spectrum of colour. Everyone knows there are colours which exist above and beyond our range of seeing. The pure vision of colour is an intricate interchange of presence and absence which speaks to the sensitive soul through the language of feeling, just as music can speak to the heart and soul where words fail. Colour has the same ability, have you ever gazed upon a sunset and wanted to drink into your soul the magnificence of the colour. Its gift is the realisation of beauty. The language of colour is both subtle and powerful at the same time and is the voiceless articulation of the divine.

In depth studies of ancient scriptures and classic works of literature concluded that early man, may not have perceived the world in the same way we do now! The philosopher Xenophanes 50 B.C describes in his writings of a time when man could not see colours in nature at all, but only in shades of light and darkness.

Our ability to perceive colour has developed as the human species has evolved. It is consciousness itself that enables the capacity to experience and perceive existence. G. Heard speaking of the evolution of conscious-ness expresses that our ability to see colours is expanding. In the old testament the rainbow is described as consisting of only three colors, red, orange, and yellow. Even Aristotle referred to the rainbow only having three colours. Yet as we gaze upon the interaction of a drop of rain and the jewel of light, which creates the rainbow, we see not three but seven visible colours. I am sure this has always been the case, what has changed is our capacity to perceive it.

Therefore, if we were to project ahead in time, it may be highly likely that people in the future will see many more colours than is possible for our generation now at this stage of evolution. We should never mistake our capacity to see something as being a limit to all there is. Colour can and does affect us on many levels of our being, especially the way we feel about what we see. It has an impact upon our:

- **Emotions**

- **Perceptions**

- **Physical body**

- **Spiritual self**

Research and studies done over many years have found that colour affects our mood, particularly in those who are sensitive. Colour has a power to affect the way we feel about what we see. An entire room painted red would ultimately impact upon the body; the heart rate would increase, a feeling of tension or anxiety would be experienced and our perceptual awareness of the space around us would alter. A red room will look much smaller than the same room decorated in a soft blue, which by contrast would create a sense of spaciousness and calm. As red is always classed as an active colour, so blue is by contrast considered passive.

Understanding the universal language of colour is a tool which enables the developing sensitive to discover a whole new world of expression. Artists know unconsciously the power and effect of colour, they bring to life the divine mystery. Colour has always been a means by which to transform a mood and convey a story without the use of the spoken word. For its message is perceived by the soul and the soul responds to the voice of the spirit rather than the intellect.

Our thoughts manifest as a living expression of colour, around each one of us we carry myriad shades and hues only visible to someone who has attuned themselves to this inner power. The whole story of our life, emotional responses and soul potentiality is there as an invisible cloak around us.

In the early1980's I had the privilege on several occasions of listening to the wonderful Sir George Trevelyan speak. He was a pioneer in conscious living, founder of the Wrekin Trust, an educational charity concerned with promoting the spiritual nature of man and the universe as part of a world-wide movement towards planetary transformation. Sir George would often stopover in Aberdeen on his travels to the Findhorn Foundation, which he was very involved in helping in its early days.

The first time I listened to Sir George speak I never heard a word he actually said, as I was so enraptured by the dance of colours that emanated from the vibration of every word he uttered. He was such a charismatic orator and came alive with passion for the topic upon which he was speaking, I couldn't help but gaze in wonder at the shifting colours that moved before my awareness. I wondered to myself if everybody present had witnessed the magic I had perceived that evening. It later became apparent that not everyone experienced the movement of colour in the way I had, I believe that being in the presence of someone so spiritually aware had in some way touched me on the level of my soul and had consequently opened the door of my own perception and the memory of the colours I used to frequently see as a child came flooding back to me.

The mystery of colour can easily be revealed but it is first necessary to awaken your spiritual powers of perception. When rightly used, these become an innate tool by which to perceive the world around us, with the totality of our awareness and a means to understand more deeply those who we share the journey of life with. The language of the spirit always conveys the distilled essence of truth.

There have been countless books written on the interpretation of colour and in the process of learning something new we have always been taught to look outside ourselves for all the answers. However, this is one area where it is necessary to solely trust our inner experience. To truly perceive the aura and convey its deeper meaning it is necessary to engage in a spontane-ous interaction with the colours as each shade reveals itself. To rely upon a book once read and refer to someone else's interpretation of this inner language would mean we become disengaged and end up repeating dead words which have no life of their own. It is important to express the living word, to do so means we enter a world of wonder and the true meaning is revealed, but if we fail to immerse ourselves all that can be discovered will remain hidden. Ultimately what then happens is we are no longer present within the moment and instead invite the intellect and the power of our rational mind to intervene.

The aura is an electromagnetic energy field that eminates from a person. It is simply our inner life our thoughts and feelings translated into the language of energy and colour which surrounds us. In fact, all living things have an aura, even trees and flowers but then all life has consciousness. The word aura derives from Latin and simply means air, the origin of which stems from Ancient Greek and means breath. The light of the soul shines through the eyes, this is why the eyes are called "the windows of the soul", and can be felt both within and without. The inner-self radiates the colours and pulse of our thoughts.

Nowadays to believe in the reality of the auric field is more acceptable due to pioneering researchers such as Walter Kilner, who invented the 'Kilner screen', which enabled a person to perceive the 'human atmosphere' as he called it. Using a substance called dicyanin dye, he was able to exclude all the other light rays and render visible ultra-violet, the result of which made the emanations of the aura more perceptible. His findings concluded disease manifested first on the auric field before it developed on the body. Following in Kilner's footsteps was Semyon Kirlian, someone who also challenged the sceptical minds and promoted the truth of the invisible. Kirlian, who was of Armenian descent and a Soviet scientist, became recognised for his 'Kirlian' photography which depicted the corona, or the light's rays, emanating from all living things.

The renaissance artists frequently portrayed religious figures as having a golden halo of light around their heads. An intuitive acknowledgment of their spiritual attainment. As all the yellow tones reflect the influence of our mental functioning, the very intensity of its hue, is indicative of their enlightenment, portrayed by the vibration of gold.

PERCEIVING THE AURA

Firstly, it is necessary to embrace the auric field as a reality and to also recognise that the aura has many levels. How can you ever really know, then, at what level you may be perceiving the aura? The answer is simple - by setting the intent to perceive at each specific level. A universal principle is energy will always follow thought.

Perceiving the colours with our spiritual senses requires nothing other than a passive mind and the ability to trust wholeheartedly all the colours and impressions experienced, allowing yourself to move inwardly with each vibration. You may see, feel, sense or even hear the word a colour has an association with. Mistakenly people fail to fully comprehend the necessity to replace the concept of 'seeing' with 'perceiving', as far as being aware of the aura is concerned. It is not realistically possible to perceive the aura with our physical eyes as our range of vision is limited. Only the capacity to see anything at the vibratory level of matter is possible with our eyes, anything above or beyond this level requires a heightened perception, the ability to perceive at faster vibrational frequencies. Therefore, it is first necessary to engage our spiritual powers of awareness, which are limitless.

To refrain from thinking is the key. If you are drawn to understanding the language of colour, I would suggest you begin by creating your own work-book, contemplate the feelings which arise as you gaze upon the vibrancy of a red rose or a soft blue delphinium. Ask yourself the question, how does it make you feel? How does each colour rest upon your spirit? Go out into nature and allow your sensitivity to be touched by the variety of hues which make up the rich canvas of life. Become so in tune that the hidden harmonies speak to your soul. Allow yourself to connect with everything in nature in order to foster the capacity to perceive the essence; forget all the man-made labels of everything you have ever been taught and be at one. Each season lends itself to a living testimony of colour; the vibrant new growth in the spring expressed in a symphony of green, in all its variation of hues, the multiplicity of the spectrum of colours is summer's divine breath as a living palette of colour and the grand finale of a rich splendour of berries in autumnal tones and a blaze of crimsons and golds, a feast for the soul. Winter's darkness harbours the power of its silent language, in preparation of awakening a cycle of continuity in the spring.

NATURE'S PALETTE

Work with blending colours on a palette, until a deeper intrinsic meaning becomes apparent, by creating your own catalogue of meanings you will have your own interpretation rather than someone else's.

When viewing the aura is it important to try to describe each colour as it touches your perception. As you begin, aim to be as specific as possible as this will enable you to truly understand the language of colour, from a soul level. To make a statement that you are aware of green is too generic, as there are hundreds of shades or tones of each colour. Alternatively, by indicating that you are aware of lime or emerald green gives the receiver an exact sense of what is being experienced and locates your attention fully within the process.

Everyone's capacity to perceive the aura will vary according to the level of spiritual awareness and understanding. When we meet a person for the very first time, there is a deep sense of how we feel in that person's presence. At an unconscious level the auric field has been translated through the language of energy and a glimpse of the person's true nature has been revealed, often before a word is even spoken, as energy cannot lie. Consequently, it is how the individual perceiving it responds to the language and meaning of colour which is relevant.

However even though the interpretation of meaning is personal to the person experiencing it, there are key meanings related to each vibration. It is for the individual to expand upon, within each given opportunity and with as much detail as is available within the experience. Each colour really does have its own unique character, just like people, and its own life.

Since all colours derive from the three primary colours it is generally thought that most people have a 'key colour' and this will essentially be a constant vibrational expression of their auric emanation.

THE THREE PRIMARIES

These arise from the trinity of spirit, body, and mind. Red always represents the body, the physical reality. Blue by contrast speaks of the spirit, the spacious and ether. Yellow represents the mind and intellect, knowledge. The apex of human attainment is a perfect balance in which we all strive to attain the balance of body, spirit and mind.

RED

Relates to the physical body, heart, reproductive system

Ruby red;   energetic, competitive, strong willed, powerful personality

Cranberry red;   grounded, realist, ambitious, survival orientated, materialistic

Volcanic red;   mentally strong, opinionated, overbearing, forceful

Rose pink;   unconditional love, compassionate, caring sensitive, giving

ORANGE

Relates to health, spleen

Sunset orange; adventurous, outgoing, courageous, magnanimous

Apricot orange; creative, intelligent, detail-orientated, self-analytical, fun loving

Coral orange; healing power, organiser, confident

YELLOW

Relates to mental abilities, intellect, solar plexus

Primrose yellow; lacking in confidence, inconsistent, indecisive, insecure

Sunshine yellow; confident, mental clarity, focused, aptitude for

learning, pragmatic

Gold;   rarely seen, spiritually aware, inspired, contemplative, universalist

Sandstone brown/yellow; dependable, reliable

GREEN

Relates to heart and lungs

Emerald green; empathic, balanced, giving, good listeners

Jade green;   creative, gentle, kind, considerate, open

Forrest green;   self-absorbed, envious, jealous, inflexible

Lime green;   communicative, adaptable, highly creative

BLUE

Relates to throat and thyroid

Sapphire blue;   truthful, innovative, mediumistic, perceptive, visionary, religious

Powder blue;   clarity, unassuming, self-conscious, artistic,imaginative, honest

Turquoise;   good communicators, idealistic, natural teachers, integrity

Navy blue;   Anxious, worriers, negative, self-contained, non-expressive

INDIGO

Relates to the brow and pituitary gland.

Highly intuitive, intense, deep emotions, someone who has overcome a lot of difficulties in life, Seership. This colour is unique, as there is only one shade of indigo with no variation in hue. To assess if it is a true indigo is easy, if you place blue next to indigo it will look purple and if you compare it to purple it will appear blue.

VIOLET

Relates to the crown, pineal gland and nervous system.

Lavender;   spiritually motivated, creative, sensitive, day dreamer, expressive

Amethyst;   far seeing, balanced, altruistic, other worldly, impracti cal, highly sensitive

Aubergine;   suppressive, controlling, drawn to ritual and ceremony, very intense.

Notice how a dominance of red tones transforms the meaning of the colour. Where the lavender and violets are positive due to its balance of blue.

ADDITIONAL COLOURS

Silver;   Adaptable, receptive to innovative ideas and ways of thinking. Thrives on variety, quick thinking

Steel grey;   fearful, negative, inflexible

White;   purity of intent, perfectionist, attainment on a spiritual level

Brown   earth tones; reliable, trustworthy, dependable, nurturing

The above colour interpretations are a gentle indication, which can lead to a more in-depth meaning, if time and effort are applied in exploring the language of colour. There are endless shades of colour within the spectrum of colour.

When viewing the aura, a general rule is the light to medium hues normally reflect positive aspects of a colour and with the intense dark ones more of the negative traits apply. It is very similar to an astrological chart whereby the planets represent both positive and negative elements. A soft mid-green may portray someone who has a very giving, caring, balanced nature, whereas someone with a much more intense dark green would have the same potentiality as the first, but is not quite in rhythm with their life, or at home in themselves.

When perceiving the spiritual aura, the colours seen at this level usually radiate a pure untainted hue, frequently soft pastel shades that are almost transparent.

It is important to look at the relationship one colour has with the next, this is significant and tells a greater story, which relates to the whole. Any one colour should never be perceived in isolation for attention should be given to how the colours blend together as a whole.

We grow as the tree grows,

Putting out leaves in the spring

And through it all the soul remains hidden

Adding ring upon ring upon ring.

Author unknown

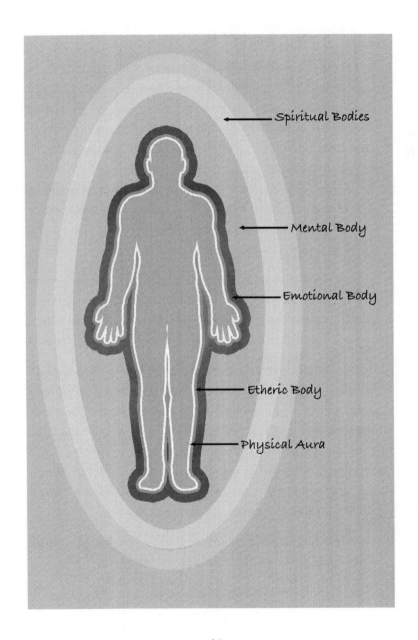

Spiritual Bodies

Mental Body

Emotional Body

Etheric Body

Physical Aura

EXERCISE

- Try visiting a sacred place such as a church or temple where for hundreds or thousands of years people have gathered together to offer their devotion and loving prayers. When you cross the threshold, allow yourself to become receptive to the atmosphere. If the energy had a colour what colour would it be? Begin to gently attune and let the vibration speak to you and a story unfold, has the vibration changed over the years? More often than not sacred buildings were built on ley lines and places where the earth's natural energy was known to converge. Try experimenting as often as you can as the more you do this the more finely tuned to the language of vibration you will become.

- Another very revealing experiment to enable you to understand the language of colour a little more deeply is to get some acrylic paints, mix the paint with just a little water. Now choose three or four colours you feel instantly drawn to, noting the colours in order of choice.

- Write down how the colours you have chosen make you feel and what you believe it reveals about yourself. Now splash a few drops of the colours you have selected onto some paper, folding the paper over, then mindfully move your hands over the paper on the folded side. When opened out should represent a symmetry picture and the colours should have blended to form a natural pattern, this can then be used by another person to interpret the story of the colours and symbols in relation to how it speaks to them about who you are.

- This simple exercise frees the mind and can be helpful by enabling the person reading the colours to relax and feel free.

- It is possible to journey through a person's entire life by perceiving the aura, and if you find a person who will willingly allow you to practise on them it can be an extremely good way of deepening your understanding.

• Begin from the very first moment the person was born and move through the colours allowing the story of their life to unfold into your awareness. Always remember if you start in a specific way, the energy created by your positivity will enable you to continue giving detailed information. It is always important to ask a person's permission first before perceiving their auric field, otherwise it can be extremely invasive. A deep responsibility and awareness of spiritual ethics should be used at all times. Remember also the auric field has many layers; the physical aura envelopes the entire physical body and is described as the level which is closest to the vibration of matter and is considered to be the only level which can be perceived with the physical eyes because of this.

THE PHYSICAL AURA

Ask the person you are viewing to stand with a white background behind them, fix your gaze on the person, look away and then look back once more focusing entirely with the intent of perceiving the physical aura. You may begin to see a soft shimmering, normally just about two centimetres from the body. If the person is in good health the aura normally appears as a silver blue colour, any areas of disease may be viewed by a slowing down or density in the energy and a change in the colour. In most countries it is not now considered acceptable practice to diagnose, just in case of incorrect diagnosis, so stay within the realms of only saying what is appropriate; if you are experimenting in a teaching environment it is necessary to make this point clear. Diagnosis, with the best will in the world, should really be left only to those in the medical profession although there have been some remarkable healers in the past who could diagnosis with incredible accuracy.

Many years ago, I was giving a very nervous gentleman an evidential read-ing and he seemed particularly uptight. At the end I asked him if he was alright, to which he asked if I could tell him if he was going to die soon with a heart attack. He explained that he had been to someone else who had told him that he 'had a massive hole' in his heart chakra and would 'very likely die soon from a heart condition'! The poor man had been worrying constantly because of this and to say something of this nature was not only completely irresponsible, but the cause of considerable anxiety. The role of a medium or healer is surely to bring reassurance and encouragement not to fill people with fear. Never will the spirit world impress you to say something, in whatever way you are working, that would inflict suffering on another.

EMOTIONAL AURA/BODY

It is normally true to say the emotional body contains within its vibration the story of a person's life. It is a reflection of how we think, feel and respond to the varying circumstances we experience. All our habitual behavioural responses are visible at this level as well as our core personality and the emerging pattern seen as trends within our life.

MENTAL AURA/BODY

This aura is more intensely seen around the head and is a projection of our mental capacities and intellectual abilities. Normally experienced as a shade of yellow, although other colours can occur, and indicates our mental functioning from the bright luminosity of the golden yellow of an inspirational highly motivated person, to the more insipid yellow of a person lacking in confidence who hasn't formed strong mental clarity and is always dependent upon the opinions of others.

SPIRITUAL AURA/BODY

Often considered to be the finest layer of the auric field and is an outer band of colour. Unlike the emotional aura, colours at this level will change the least during the course of a lifetime, as real spiritual progression is rarely quick because it necessitates the ability to overcome what is often classed as limiting behaviours and patterns. Working on yourself as a spiritual being is often a slow process. This level Is the farthest away from the body and reveals spiritual growth and the potential abilities of the soul.

INTERTWINING LEVELS, THE ETHERIC BODY.

The etheric body completely surrounds the physical form and has often been referred to as our etheric double, it is also considered to be a meeting place of spiritual and physical levels. It has three main functions and is described as being in turn a receiver, assimilator and transmitter of what is often referred to in Sanskrit and in the world of yoga as 'prana'. Prana is considered to be the life force which vitalises all creation, as energy is absorbed through the etheric body through a network of energy centres, where it is then utilised to sustain our glands and nervous system and then distributed throughout the body, in the process energising the physical self.

CONTEMPLATING INNER MEANINGS

What colour comes to mind when you contemplate the word 'birth'? Repeat the word a few times connecting with your deepest self and then do the same with the word 'death'; allow the colour to arise in your awareness. How does it make you feel and why do you think of a specific colour? This can be incredibly revealing. Now consider for contemplation the word 'love'; become receptive to the colours which naturally drift into your awareness and allow the inner meaning to reveal itself to you.

EXPERIMENT:

- *In a group of people, work in pairs and before you start exploring any ability to perceive the aura, begin by inviting each person to describe to a partner the colour red, how it makes them feel but without engaging thinking. Secondly ask the pairs to try describing blue in the same manner.*

- *Now discuss any observations. Normally what is experienced is the volume of noise goes up when red is being described and any talking becomes louder and faster, yet the complete opposite will happen when describing blue as the volume becomes much softer and far gentler.*

- *This is such a lovely exercise and beautifully demonstrates the power and effect colour can have on us all.*

THE HIDDEN MEANING OF LIGHT

"For the rest of my life I want to reflect, on what light is".

Albert Einstein

The mystic who was known by the name of both Jesus and Issa, is quoted as saying "the light of the body is the eye; therefore, thine eye be single, thy whole body shall be full of light". Matthew 6:22. If you will, permit me to go on a journey of possibility for a moment and ask the question, what if the prophet was referring to the third eye often frequently associated with the seat of inner seeing and vision? If so, a whole new world of insight reveals itself. When we perceive through the eye of the spirit all are one.

The deeper implication is incredibly profound. When we experience unity consciousness, all are equal, there is no outside, no separation, no them or us! The eye is frequently symbolic of, and synonymous with, inner consciousness because this is the very essence of the universe and the lens of perception. If the only thing we see is oneness, we are indeed full of light. Surely this is the real teaching of the prophet, after all Jesus wasn't even a Christian but was born into Judaism. Christianity did not become a recognised religion until two hundred and fifty years later. Jesus taught a universal message of unconditional love, beyond all the labels which separate and divide. His mission was to be a bridge between heaven and earth, in the truest sense of the word Jesus was what is now commonly called a medium. Similar to a great deal of trance teachings, when he was moved by the power, he spoke using the universal language of parables or metaphors. In fact, he referred frequently to the idea that we are all divine, born of a living God, "is it not written in your Law, 'I have said you are "gods"' (John 10; 31-34). It couldn't be said in plainer language each one of us, without exception, shares a common divinity. Even though some still deny this truth, which is invariably the result of religious conditioning or a subconscious need to remain without responsibility, the church has deified Jesus. What was his real message? Maybe we too, can find out if we sit in the silence.

The distilled essence of Jesus's wisdom has been tragically lost during the centuries and little comprehended. But mystics are very rarely understood and the majority of the world has yet to catch a glimpse of their vision. If humanity collectively realised their divinity, it would consequently lead to an acceleration of growth on all levels of our being with people beginning to think for themselves in complete freedom. Just imagine how much could be achieved and how the world would reap the benefit if all peoples moved forward in this way. Sadly, until now, many world religions have governed by fear and the faith of love has often been lost. Yet a new dawn is rising and mankind is turning towards the light of truth at last!

There are supposedly accounts in the remotest monasteries in Tibet of the man from Nazareth who sought council and direction from the learned spiritual teachers of their day and from Indian Yogis. Jesus' spiritual gifts didn't suddenly manifest overnight, instead he learned how to commune with higher realms, was taught how to meditate and be at one with the power of the spirit. "I can of myself do nothing; the father which dwelleth in me doeth the works", by this very statement Jesus was declaring, just like each of us in this present day who serves as a medium or a healer knows, we are just a channel and all we can ever really learn is how to inwardly move with this power and become proficient at becoming one with it. The potential to recognise this power as an aspect of our own self arises from a deep intuitive knowledge of our own true nature; sadly, the living of life, the need to conform and a consequent need to label everyone and everything has enabled people to forget who they really are and their divine heritage. The problem is if we aren't aware of our divinity, we can't claim it as our own. Jesus recognised this to be true and consequently tried his best to make us realise and become aware. There is a beautiful saying of a baby before being born, crying 'please don't let me forget who I really am' and in the process of being born says 'help I am already forgetting'!

It is apparent more than ever before that what is emerging in these current times is a new concept of God, as the Trappist Monk, Thomas Keating, so aptly said, "We can no longer accept a God that is someone else". How insightful and visionary is this incredibly realistic quote. Not bound by the traditional path of viewing God, Thomas Keating was thinking alive to the present moment and the needs of today and spoke the language of the heart.

There exists a lineage of love which has tenderly touched those from every epoch, its reach surpasses culture, class and is regardless of religious denomination. There are accounts of Jesus appearing to St Francis of Assisi, and countless mystics, including Therese Neumann, St Teresa of Avila, Sri Ramakrishna, Emmanuel Swedenborg, Padre Pio, and Andrew Jackson Davis, who was considered to be the 'father of the philosophy of spiritualism'. The latter was visited also by Emmanuel Swedenborg. We are never left wanting, for those who have gone before us in the world unseen are always close enough to inspire and enlighten. Their message can be heard still in the souls of those who are truly awake.

What has the above got to do with the auric field, you may be thinking. There is a direct link, as Jesus may well have been one of our greatest mystics and mediums, for he demonstrated all the gifts of the spirit, long before the birthdate of modern spiritualism. How did he choose his followers? As he gazed upon them, he knew by the light of their aura; here were people who had reached a place in their spiritual evolution who would receive the teachings of the spirit and by the grace of receiving be so touched they would become empowered to spread the word, long after his physical presence had gone.

For over two and a half thousand years after his presence upon the earth Jesus' teachings are remembered, even though frequently misunderstood. True spiritual teachers prepare the way for those who walk behind, but have we developed the capacity to comprehend the language of the eternal?

Are you a god? They asked the buddha.

No, he replied.

Are you an angel then?

No, a saint, no!

Then what are you?

To which the buddha replied,

I am purely and simply awake!

Reference:

The Human Atmosphere by Walter Kilner, Create Space Independent Publishing Platform.

Catching the light: The Entwined History of Light and Mind by Arthur Zajonc, Oxford University Press

The Unknown life of Jesus Christ by Nicolas Notovitch, Forgotten Books

Further reading:

The Gift of Healing: The Story of Lilley the Healer by Arthur Keith-Desmond, Psychic Press

CHAPTER FIVE

THE NATURE OF COMMUNICATION

_____   _____

Goodbyes are only for those who love with their eyes.

Because for those who love with heart and soul

there is no such thing as separation.

Rumi.

The desire to communicate flows naturally from those who have passed. After all there is so much to convey and share, wouldn't we all be the same? Don't grieve for me must be their heart-felt message. How it must pain them to realise they are our source of suffering. Yes of course they miss us, "Parting is such sweet sorrow", as William Shakespeare so aptly expressed it but, in their reality, there is no such thing as 'time' and we will be reunited in the beat of a heart. It is only we who still, immersed in the limitations of the body and the experience of linear existence, endure the slow passage of time.

Our sorrow springs not just from a newly opened wound, but the soul's memory of our eternal home, and not just from a sense of separation, for our tears are born from a sense of homesickness and longing; it is we who are away from home and who have been left behind. As the metaphysical poet Henry Vaughan expressed in his poem, "They are all gone into the world of light, whilst I am left lingering here". The deeper self has been reminded of this truth, our loved one's passing has for them been the doorway to their eternal home and now all we can do is wait until the time comes when we shall be reunited.

Yet even though the soul hungers for the presence of those we have loved they do not cease to exist, not for one moment. Their life continues with a heightened capacity to love more fully and to experience reality with a new-found sense of freedom. So often it has been expressed that they watch over us still and their footsteps walk in rhythm with our own if we but knew. This new freedom and power allows them, when a need arises, to be present with us - loving us more abundantly than before.

How easy is it for those in the spirit world to communicate? I have often asked myself this very question, yet if the spirit people are able to convey anything to us regarding their reality it is necessary to do so in a way that embodies not their experience but ours. Because we must navigate our experience through our framework of reality, it must make it difficult for them to relay all the wonders of their new existence. Often in the history of communication, those in the spirit world have conveyed how they find language and the limitations of the mind of the medium sometimes restrains their efforts.

It is a possibility that those some would call dead have a far greater intensity of perception and other means to sense reality of which we know, or can remember, nothing at all. The spirit world, invisible to ordinary vision, touches spiritual vision. Where is this other world? You may well ask. As the renowned physicist and pioneering spiritualist Sir Oliver Lodge once stated, "reality is to be found only in the invisible". We only receive one billionth, of the information out there in the universe, all the rest is edited out and the brain acts as a filter, otherwise we would all be experiencing overload. Our nervous systems may be amplifiers of consciousness, improving our capacity to experience the world. The five senses are a means by which we perceive material reality, but for every physical sense we have there exists its spiritual equivalent. However, it is probably true to say there are even vaster and higher means of experiencing, which we currently have no earthly language to describe.

Intuition is a faculty whereby an integration with infinite consciousness can be experienced, it predominately paves the way for, and is related to, a deep sense of interconnection. It can be likened to listening to the heart rather than the head, learning from within rather than without and enables a direct perception of truth. To awaken our intuitive nature is like opening a door which facilitates the remembrance of our true nature, the spirit.

Ways of perceiving with our spiritual faculties, associated within mediumistic experience, are commonly known as the 'Clair Senses'. Clair being of French origin and simply meaning 'clear'. This definition includes any or all types of experiencing beyond the five senses on a metaphysical level, our spiritual senses function at a subtler level and yet with gentle effort and training can become more heightened and a means to perceive the spirit world.

- **Clairvoyance;** clear seeing

- **Clairsentience;** clear sensing

- **Clairaudience;** clear hearing

- **Claircognizance;** clear knowing

- **Clairolfactory;** clear smelling

- **Clairgustance;** clear tasting

Although defined in such a manner, this does little to fully describe the heightened state of awareness and the sensation of being immersed in a spiritual 'oneness' that the Clair Senses impart. There is a feeling of being more fully alive, awakening a power that lives within us and can transform our experience of reality and our capacity to perceive the wonders of existence.

A question frequently asked is 'what's the difference between someone who is a psychic and someone who is a medium?', in the words of Gordon Higginson "All mediums are psychic, but not all psychics are mediums". This describes the distinct difference between the two. A psychic will tell the story of the person here upon the earth, a medium the story of the spirit. Mediumship depends more upon spiritual growth and awareness than our psychic faculties, essentially it is contact with higher worlds.

The astronaut Edgar Mitchell, who was on the space shuttle Apollo 14 in 1974, after spending 33 hours on the moon was making the homeward journey after his mission when he witnessed the astonishing sight of all the planets in alignment as the space shuttle rotated. He was so in awe and deeply moved by what he saw that he had, what he described as, a profound spiritual experience which changed his life and his views regarding the meaning of existence. This can be likened to 'samadhi'; a mystical experience where all existence appears as one vast whole, accompanied by a blissful state of awareness. The experience made him re-direct his life to explore the realms of consciousness. Inspired by his new insight, he went on to establish the Noetic Science Organisation. What I find thought provoking is Edgar's concept that intuition, rather than being the sixth sense by which it is commonly known, is really our first sense as it belongs to our spiritual self and is our true means of experiencing reality.

Intuition, or pure knowing, is an inherent quality of the soul and is a valuable part of mediumistic development. The more we remember to trust the language of intuition the easier it becomes to tap into our spiritual resources. Intuitive connection needs to be encouraged in the early stages of mediumistic unfoldment. It requires a deep ability to inwardly engage in listening beyond the distractions of the mind as the nature of the mind is such that it will always try to interrupt and create doubts regarding our abilities.

The solar plexus is considered to be the brain of our nervous system and the reason why we intuitively feel something, which is often classed as 'a gut feeling'. Learning to trust what we experience viscerally is an important part of our mediumistic journey. For where does this ability to truly know something arise, other than the spirit? For the dialogue of the spirit has always been the language of feeling, we just have to remind ourselves to trust and, in trusting, to listen.

Every thought we have ever entertained and believed to be true is sent by our brain to the solar plexus, our abdominal brain, and is brought into our world as a reality. All the habitual thought patterns are stored in our sub conscious mind, and ultimately manifest in our life. In nearly every spiritual tradition there is emphasis on the need to school our minds into thinking in a life enhancing way. When developing mediumistic power, it is so important to cultivate a positive mental attitude and the concentrative abilities of the mind.

Observing is a means to learn and provides a valuable lesson in which development blossoms. It is beneficial to just purely and simply witness other mediums when they are moving into the power and presence of the spirit, as the art of simply paying attention can teach so much. I remember as though it was only yesterday the sheer joy of watching those masters of the gift of mediumship, how, with such a skillful art, they gracefully moved into perceiving other dimensions of existence. Within the beat of a heart, it was as though a once empty room now not only filled with people of the physical kind but was now charged with a bountiful abundance of spirit guests. How did it all happen? Just as a poet finds a language to convey the mysteries and wonders of existence, a medium sublimely engages in a present moment conversation with someone who has left behind the physical form and can attune to all the many characters that have made up that life.

What is helpful in the role of the medium is looking at the experience from the spirit person's perspective. How would you define yourself? What qualities or habits separate you from everyone else or convey enough conclusive information to enable you to be recognisable? What could you say? This gives a deeper sense of meaning and purpose. Retaining the awareness that those who communicate through you are still real people, with human emotions and relationships, who have lived a material life is essential. To never lose sight of this will serve you well throughout the highs and lows of the mediumistic journey.

YOU CAN'T EXPERIENCE WHAT YOU DON'T BELIEVE

Love is the bridge between heaven and earth and the development of mediumship necessitates a deep sense of belief in yourself as much as the spirit world. It is important always to start a communication from a place of possibility rather than doubt. A mistake frequently made in the early days of mediumistic development is to try too hard, this will disable rather than enable, as mediumship flourishes when the mind is free from tension and expectation. Excessive effort creates a rigidity which will ultimately negate the efforts made by those who are making attempts to communicate. A mind resting in stillness, allowing your focus and attention to move gently to the breath, will help foster the right conditions and of course a large sprinkling of belief.

It is important as a medium to bring life to the presence of the spirit as they are alive, to bring them home to their loved ones is the true grace of communication, to this end a medium should endeavour to relay with integrity and true sensitivity the beauty of the communication. There exists a vast difference between describing the spirit person and becoming them, of course this occurs in a subtle yet real way and is mediumship functioning at its very best, as there is no trying involved.

It is a privilege to be able to convey the thoughts and message of hope and a love unchanged by the process of death of the physical body. Yet nothing happens without the spirit person's co-operation and with immense effort behind the scenes taking place, in order for the medium to successfully convey all that is classed as proof of survival.

Breath is a key, we are born to the physical world and come into this life on the breath and we go out on the breath. The English word "spirit" comes from the Latin spiritus, which means breath. For every mediumistic state of awareness there is an appropriate change in the rhythm of the breath. For our whole life the breath has been breathing us. Just as movement of the tide is governed by the cycle of the moon, the spirit moves this inner rhythm inherent in man.

MUSICIAN OF THE SOUL

When does the moment occur which shapes the inner experience that gives life to a communication and how does the medium inwardly move with their awareness from being conscious of this physical reality to the next, of the presence of the spirit? What frames our experience and gives birth to the wonder of a communication?

Have you ever observed a musician when their whole being becomes an extension and living expression of the music? How every note impacts the physical self which responds with tender synchronicity to the rhythm. When a musician plays in this way it is as though the person can no longer be found, for they become one with the sound; mediumship is the same, for both the musician and the medium are lost in the art of forgetting the self, becoming one with the music of existence.

Just as the quality of the music can only be as good as both the natural abilities of the musician and the instrument being played upon, so too does the spirit communicator relay information to varying degrees and levels depending upon the sensitivity of the medium.

To have a mind that is as free as the trees being moved by the direction of the wind on a summer's day, the medium's mind must be flexible so that they can, within the breath of a moment, move fleetingly from one awareness to another.

Each heart beats to a different rhythm and so does the way in which we all perceive the world differ. We carry within our soul a unique ability to enrich the world, to view life from a distinct perspective which responds to every changing moment of life. No two people share the same universe, no one ever sees another's experience, our perception of reality is framed by our conditioning and expectations and will therefore colour "how we see, what we see".

How then can the communication be defined by uniformity, when by its very nature is free, within the grace of each moment and person communicating. We are in danger of destroying that which is both beautiful and unique within the nature of mediumistic expression by over-schooling.

Learn to listen to those in the world unseen, to allow yourself to be the conduit. For any effort on the part of the medium to make sense of the information or understand will cause the mind to interfere and make a judgment. Once this happens the natural flow of the information will be interrupted. It is a common mistake to think that as a medium it is your job to 'interpret' the information but to do this could mean you may 'misinterpret'. Your goal should be to give exactly what you receive using your spiritual powers of awareness. This experience is simplified by the phrase, 'If you begin to think you will lose the link', where the danger is of allowing your mind to begin to try to make sense of the communication. Remember this, as it is not only important, but vital.

Potential mediumistic ability is enhanced by the realisation that the subconscious mind needs to be subdued or pacified so no interference can disturb what would otherwise be a natural flow of communication. To master the art and ability to differentiate between what is your own mental meanderings and what is extraneous thought flow coming from a spirit person is vital. Feeling not only gives life to the experience but helps instill a deep sense of realisation that what is happening is authentic.

When beginning to explore your own mediumistic powers of awareness it is important to realise each person will respond to the influence of the spirit world in a unique manner. Basically, there exists two schools of thought regarding communication and it is easy to get confused and what starts out a natural ability ends up being coerced into something unnatural.

TO ASK OR NOT TO ASK, THAT IS THE QUESTION?

One school of thought is to 'ask' the spirit communicator and the other is simply to 'allow' the spirit to relay the information uninterrupted. In my experience what works best is the latter, this enables the spirit person to decide what is essential to convey. My reasons are that if you 'ask' it engages your own mind and therefore the mind searches for an answer and could interrupt the flow of communication. I am sure within the spirit person's awareness they must have a sense of what it is necessary to communicate in order for them to be identifiable and if we interfere surely it will make what they are aiming to achieve inaccessible. When a question is asked our mind is active, when we become the conduit the mind is passive, yet receptive. Mediumship requires the divine, feminine principle of receptivity. It is, after all, the spirit communicator's story not the medium's so we should always respect their right to convey whatever information they feel is relevant and meaningful.

Instead of asking a direct question of the spirit it is more conducive to ask a question of your awareness, inviting your attention to focus more fully on whatever the spirit communicator is trying to relay. Often people have a misconception that to see the spirit is the best way of experiencing the communication, but I believe it is through the language of feeling that the spirit people really come to life and you can begin to truly experience them as a living presence! Seeing only conveys a tiny essence of who they are. Yet through the power of sensing and feeling an entire story has the potential to be conveyed.

I believe the intelligence and depth of the information the spirit convey often goes unnoticed by those who receive it, due to the excitement of the moment and a lack of realisation of just how one simple communication on closer analysis reveals layers upon layers of meaning.

FOUNDATION FOR COMMUNICATING

Perception is as much active and creative, as it is passive and receptive. Once you have made an offering to the spirit world that you might perceive their presence, on becoming aware of a spirit person it is fundamental to get to know who they are, the very same way we would find out about someone we have just met for the first time as the same concept applies to the spirit. Although I must add it is important to do this without entering into the head, as if you locate your attention in your head, you will stay in your head. Your mediumship will flourish best if you begin by listening deeply to your awareness.

If you can, you should meet the spirit person in and through the language of your sensitivity and then just allow your spiritual power of perception to speak for itself. This opens up an opportunity to experience a deep sense of who they are and creates an interconnectedness.

Getting to know the spirit person is paramount to sustaining a communication, one which evolves from the energy generated by trust. The communication then follows a natural direction from those in the spirit world and as long as the medium continues to engage with the communicator this will enable an energetic connection to be maintained a little similar to a phone line. Once the connection has been made, as long as the medium doesn't put the phone down and disconnect the spirit by forgetting to mention them or hold their focus, so much can be achieved. The very act of mentioning who it is keeps the energy freely flowing from spirit to medium and a cycle of energy continues. If we forget to mention the spirit person it makes it far more difficult for them and it's something very similar to switching the electricity off, as to do so means we will have to go to the effort to switch it back on again in order to reconnect the source of power.

Fundamental to a good communication is to be aware of not bringing too much in the way of expectations into the experience. If we give ourselves too much pressure, we will come from the head space rather than the heart and will be in danger of over-trying, which is never conducive to a good communication.

If you ever get a 'no' response from the person you are trying to read for, don't allow a 'no' to put you off or make you start doubting what you have been experiencing; instead invite a no to be the opportunity to experience the information in more depth. By viewing the response from a positive rather than a negative perspective, will help you maintain the communication.

Never take the communication too personally even if on a particular occasion you view your practice as not having worked or flowed very well. Remember it may also be the spirit person's very first attempt at communicating. I believe they have to learn as much as we do the art of communicating, as it is an art and, like any crafts person, all the appropriate tools of the trade must be learnt in order to achieve the best possible outcome for all concerned. So many varying qualities contribute to a communication reaching its potential.

Identifying with the outcome too much will lead you to seriously get caught up with the ego and, ultimately, begin to listen to the judgments made by the mind and even worse other people. Other people may judge, let them it's human nature after all, just don't allow yourself to get immersed in the opinions of others. As a medium your job is to listen to the spirit. If you can master this you will save yourself a great deal of mental anguish and of course, you will never end up being a slave to the ego. Cultivate the art of being gracefully detached, this will enable you to be the best channel you can be.

If electricity is the means to bring light and power to this world, love is the same to the world of spirit communication. To begin from a place of positive power will enhance the connection with the spirit world; they require of each medium to bring their best self and to begin always from an inward place of love and belief, as this will reflect in the quality of power within the communication.

As touched upon earlier, as a medium it is best to leave it to the spirit to sort out what needs to be conveyed, although to be able to embody the essence and presence of the spirit is mediumship at its finest, for it is not the medium's job to find out what needs to be said, this is up to the spirit and if left to their own devices they will soon come up with facts and information which is meaningful to the person who receives the communication. Even though information expressed may appear apparently insignificant to an observer, it is surely for the loved one who is blessed with receiving it to decide. It is true to say then that evidence is just like beauty and 'is in the eyes of the beholder'.

In the beginning it requires a great deal of natural focus of awareness by the medium to stay connected to the spirit communicator. Often it is the medium's concentration that fails rather than the spirit person ending the communication. If the medium moves their attention away too soon because they are mentally tired it is very similar to putting the phone down on someone in the middle of a conversation. In the early days of exploring any mediumistic potential it is often powers of concentration and an ability to stay focused that require to be developed more. It is important to offer an opportunity to the loved one in the spirit before bringing the communication to a close, to invite an offering by saying 'is there anything else you wish to convey?' is simple to do and can be enormously beneficial.

Years ago, it was a common expression of a medium taking a church service or public demonstration to say they could no longer work as the power had gone! Where exactly had it gone, I would wonder to myself. I would ponder considerably about this especially as, essentially, the medium is working with a limitless power. I think it would be more correct to say the medium could no longer hold their attention any more or concentrate enough to be aware of a spirit person with clarity. My conclusion was that even though the power of the spirit is limitless the physical self has its material limitations and a hot day, for instance, can without doubt affect the attention of the audience and the concentration of the medium, but never the spirit.

When a loved one has been passed over a long time it is sometimes difficult to even bring to mind with great clarity what they looked like, as our memories can fade, however we will never forget how someone made us feel. Feelings live in the soul in a way that gives powerful coherence, but our visual memory may fade and die. It makes so much sense then, that the language of feeling is often the means by which the spirit choose to express themselves. After all we are sentient beings and feelings give life to reality. For the communication to reach its potential through the medium it is important that there is a continuous thought of acceptance, this maintains the flow of energy from the spirit. Awareness at all times should be lovingly placed on the spirit and only briefly on the response of the recipient. I have learnt over the years that people may forget but the spirit never does, as their memory is not dimmed by the passing of earthly years or the stresses of life. So where are you going to place your trust?

Throughout the communication it is important to listen to the energy with your awareness; it's as though as a channel for the spirit you are capable of doing many things in one moment.

ENHANCING COMMUNICATION

The availability of the mind is required to enable an inner receptivity, followed by an offering of loving intent, then it becomes possible to encounter the generosity of silence. An interior silence always precedes an awareness of the presence of the spirit. How can those in the spirit world communicate with us if our heads are full of all the many distractions that preoccupy us today. Have you ever tried to phone someone urgently but been frustrated as the line is already busy, maybe this is like the conditions which face our loved ones when trying to reach us from the other side?

Creating a daily routine will help enormously, together with the additional realisation that as a medium you cannot work without your relationship with the unseen world. Make a daily offering of saying 'what can I do for you spirit?', or if you teach others say 'help me through your power and grace to meet both the individual and collective need of the people present'; this invites the spirit influence to become more involved and creates the possibility to touch souls and to teach in a natural way, rather than a rigid one.

A frequently asked question is, 'how do the spirit communicators know to be there?' Firstly, I believe the spirit loved ones receive our intent through the vibration of our thoughts. A thought is light energy shaped by consciousness. Every time we think, we are creating something out of light. The misconception in the past has derived from the opinion that thought is manufactured in the brain rather than the soul, but if thought originated in the brain then all thought would cease with bodily death. All thought belongs to the soul where it is a vital creative power. The word 'soul' originates from Greek and literally means sun, the soul is the spiritual sun of our eternal self. No neurologist whilst operating on the human brain has ever located a thought, only electro chemical reactions can be measured. Information is actualised in the brain but derives from the soul. In the same way as we cannot see the wind, only the effects of it.

A simple thought defies the boundaries of time and space so our desire to communicate is instantly known by those in the spirit world. The spiritual faculties function at a level above and beyond our everyday awareness making the ability to perceive other realities possible. I cannot emphasis enough the need, first of all, to cultivate a deep belief in yourself. Of all the words you say, the words you tell yourself are the most revealing and the most important. If you believe a label you have given yourself you are in danger of that limitation becoming your reality, as the mind believes what we tell ourselves about ourselves when we repeat something often enough and our beliefs contribute to defining not only our mediumistic abilities but our entire life.

Allowing yourself to embrace the concept there is no 'here' or 'there' helps enormously. These divisions are a creation of our mental concepts and the removal of these barriers make it all possible. It is a known fact that a particle of energy can exist in the same space as another particle, because each is on a different frequency. This means the spirit world can co-exist simultaneously with our world but on a different vibration although we may not be aware of their reality, as they too are not aware of ours, until by loving intent each experiences a synchronisation.

THE NEED TO UNDERSTAND THE PROCESS

How can we master something if we don't first understand it? The art of paying attention and processing each communication is immeasurable and will not only serve to help your own development but contribute towards those who are following in your footsteps by giving more insight; those in the spirit world are evolving and growing just as much as we are. Each time we communicate we are adding to a collective understanding which we leave as a treasure behind us.

It is important to allow your mediumship time to develop and not to want to be in too much of a rush. When we push for immediate results, we fail to inhabit the space which exists where an opening is created for us to learn and inner growth can take place. Of course, it is natural to feel enthusiastic, which is of course a very enriching quality, but it is always paramount to remember even though we may be bursting to explore a newly awakened awareness not everyone we meet may be ready to hear!

It is normal when giving a communication from the spirit world for the spirit person to not only relay information which is considered conclusive proof of survival, but also the reason why they have made all the effort in the first place. This part is classed as the message and it is invariably a reflection either of a need in the recipient's life or of the spirit, maybe they never got to say goodbye or some other equally important subject. Whatever it may be, it is important not to view it as a separate part but instead all as one whole. If you do this you will find an effortless flow is experienced, without even having to stop and search for a reason.

FINDING THE RIGHT TEACHER

The best teachers are really those of the spirit kind who know you better than you know yourself, but of course it is necessary to seek out those who have more experience than us, as far as knowledge is concerned. A good teacher will gently suggest possibilities, to encourage the best from each person and point the way, but never demand or tell you how you should be experiencing the information. Each person is unique and mediumistic unfoldment should be nurtured to enable a natural, not manufactured, expression of the power.

Rudolf Steiner said, "You will never be good teachers if you focus only on what you do and not upon who you are". A good teacher realises that the revealing of mediumistic powers is a journey and we never really arrive, so to make continued effort to work on yourself inwardly is the only real way to progress. It is so important that you find a teacher who you resonate with and who themselves is a good example. Once you have found one its advantageous to stay with that particular person until you have outgrown the need. I say this as there exist so many varying ways regarding the teaching of mediumship that if you try to learn from too many different people you just end up confused and tied up in a knot. However, it is worthwhile initially exploring different teachers and approaches, to find out what works for you. In the process it is good to ask yourself these healthy questions: Does the teacher make me feel comfortable within myself? Is a nurturing atmosphere being created? Can the teacher do what they are telling their students to do? Is what is being taught founded on facts that can be substantiated?

If I lie down one day and die in my sleep

How will I know if I still dream

A dream of death in life

Or a dream of life in death

That maybe I will wake again a child still dreaming

And how will I know which life I have left before sleep?

And which life I have come to on waking

Would I dream dying or die of dreaming

And is there a difference.

- Author unknown

EXERCISE.

- *Ask a friend for a photo of a relative in the spirit, now get the person the photo belongs to, to write down five or six significant things about the spirit person, they particularly remember. The more unusual the better, quirky habits, mannerisms, memories, places visited together but focusing on receiving as much detail about their presence as possible.*

- *Allow yourself to become receptive to any impressions that seem to arise within you without judgment just giving what you receive. Notice feelings or thoughts that you were not aware of earlier, trust in whatever information you are receiving, yet refraining from trying to make sense of, or understand the information.*

- *Additionally offer to the spirit the possibility that you receive something that is not currently known about the communicator, that they will have to seek validation of from another family member. This proves and discounts any theory that all the medium is doing is reading the mind of the sitter and creates a special moment of realisation for the recipient, which can create a lasting impact.*

CHAPTER SIX

OUR RICH AND DIVERSE HERITAGE

"Our mission is to spiritualise the world, to turn the attention of the

world inward to the immortality of the soul"

Gordon Higginson

The early days of modern spiritualism were filled with remarkable phenomena. When looking at these, though, it is necessary to make sure the medium
had a reputation which had earned respect and was credible before being
believed. Some of the first attempts to communicate were through what is
described as physical mediumship. For the spirit world it was necessary that,
in order to make people stop, look, and listen, the phenomena provided a
way to draw people's attention to the message they were trying to convey.
This type of mediumship is a more specialised ability and requires the
production of a substance called ectoplasm. The word ectoplasm originates
from Greek and means 'exteriorised substance'. Ectoplasm is drawn from
the medium typically via an orifice and very often the mouth. It can form as
a vaporous mist which ultimately becomes more solid in appearance and
depending upon the power and conditions provided, will vary in both quality

and quantity. It is light-sensitive and normally the reason why séances are held in the dark or with the use of a soft red light. It is through the use and manipulation of ectoplasm that physical mediumship occurs.

"What the eyes see, the mind believes" is indeed true and a good séance in the presence of a genuine medium can be viewed as breaking the boundaries of all that is conceived to be real and taking possibility to new heights. There really are no limitations within the field of physical phenomena when you have the right conditions. These consist of a good strong physical medium and a receptive group of people in an atmosphere of love, with no rigid expectations.

TYPES OF SPIRITUALIST PHENOMENA

MATERIALISATION

This can be both full and partial materialisation of a spirit loved one. Depending upon the quantity of ectoplasm produced, the spirit people can materialise and have been known to walk around the room and directly converse with their loved ones. Just as a baby in the womb's life is dependent upon the life force of the mother through the connection of the umbilical cord, so too is the spirit person dependent upon the medium and is connected in the same way through an ectoplasmic cord.

The mediumship of Alec Harris is remarkable and left no shadow of doubt as to the reality of the materialised forms. Not only did Alec have great integrity but during the demonstrations he would be seen sitting strapped to his chair, in an unconscious state, whilst in front of him two or more spirit forms would manifest, and their size and appearance would differ considerably from that of the medium.

TRANSFIGURATION

In this phenomenon a mask forms, created from the production of ectoplasm normally just a few centimetres in front of the face of the medium. The spirit communicators form their face from the ectoplasm, enabling all present to simultaneously see a creation of the spirit person's features. Many people mistakenly think a slight overshadowing of the spirit is transfiguration. To simply define the difference, it is true to say that overshadowing does not require ectoplasm whereas transfiguration does.

INDEPENDENT DIRECT VOICE

A replica voice box is formed from ectoplasm enabling the spirit to speak directly to their loved ones independent of the medium. Those in the spirit have tried to explain exactly what is required of them and have conveyed the need to concentrate their thoughts, which is then transferred into audible vibrations, through what has been referred to as an 'etheric amplifier' in order to be audibly heard by all present. Before such a phenomenon can occur, it is normal for the medium to be under a very strong influence of the spirit and often in an unconscious state. Although this is not always the case as medium Leslie Flint, however, was an exception and frequently joined in with the conversations being held when two or more spirit voices manifested. The Scottish Medium John Campbell Sloane was a very respected medium who also worked in this way and was responsible for convincing a once very sceptical Arthur Findlay of the reality of life after death. Arthur later went on to bequeath his stately home to be used on his passing as a spiritualist college, to further the progress of what he called 'Psychic Science' and assist in the development and understanding of mediumistic abilities.

Direct voice is independent of the medium, despite requiring the presence of a physical medium to provide both the power and conditions. It makes it possible for the spirit to speak to their loved ones in a different language that is unknown to the medium in their everyday awareness. This can be the means of giving the most remarkable proof.

MANIFESTATION OF APPORTS,

This phenomenon is the de-materialisation of an object followed by its re-materialisation in a different place; somewhere the spirit intends it to appear. This procedure has been described as simply the speeding up of the molecular structure of an article enabling it to pass through matter and the subsequent slowing down of its atomic structure enabling it to re appear.

LEVEITATION OF OBJECTS AND PEOPLE;

By defying the laws of gravity, the spirit world have demonstrated the reality of levitating not only objects, but in many cases the mediums themselves; such is the case with Scottish medium Daniel Dunglas Home, (1833-1886). There are many testimonies to the incredible abilities of Home, the accounts are notably all from particularly educated and respected people of their time; the list is long and includes Lords, Judges, Professors, Royalty, and all manner of investigators. The single, most famous, incident, was the much talked about event that took place at his home in London, on a cold December evening in 1868. Home was holding a séance when those in attendance witnessed the medium go into a trance state, then much to their amazement proceeded to float in the air, his body appeared to elongate before being turned by an invisible power, until he was completely horizontal, Home then gently floated out of the window of the room in which they were gathered and entered in through another window, his body still horizontal and floating effortlessly through the air. The attendees Lord Adare, Lord Lindsay and others all testified to the event that they had witnessed, even though incredible and hard for the mind to conceive! It is worthwhile mentioning here, even though many people tried hard to discredit D. D. Home, including the famous escapologist Harry Houdini, he was never once found to be cheating, even after hundreds of seances held in countless countries.

As poet and novelist, Franz Werfel, once said, "for those who believe, no explanation is necessary. For those who do not believe no explanation is possible". This statement essentially sums up the witnessing of phenomena, in a nutshell. It is apparent that however much supernormal phenomena is experienced, the rationale of the human mind will mean that some people will invariably choose to find another, more logical, explanation for it, rather than face the truth of the situation. Belief then, is not so much about encountering the miraculous, but is more a reflection of an individual's spiritual growth and a willingness to invite a whole new world of possibility into our lives.

The spirit world has the ability to produce perfumes and odours and create spirit lights so real all present can simultaneously see them. The manifestation of spirit lights has nothing to do with a person's clairvoyant vision and should be visible to all. Additionally, the spirit are able to alter the temperature in the room.

Many physical mediums have endured hardships and had their abilities scrutinised by researchers who had very little in the way of understanding as to the nature of genuine mediumship. Frequently the need to ensure that the medium could not be acting fraudulently superseded the wonder of the phenomena itself and extraordinary efforts to bind and secure the medium ensued. It was spiritualist Sir Arthur Conan Doyle who stated, "when you have eliminated the impossible whatever remains, however improbable, must be the truth". These incredible souls suffered so the world could bear witness to the truth that man survives bodily death and in order to ensure that those coming after them could experience the blessing which freedom of expression brings.

All physical phenomena proves that 'spirit is superior to matter', especially if evidence is provided and serves to support the reality and intelligence of the spirit world. Above and beyond the movement of objects or other such wonders there is an invisible team of spirit helpers making it possible. So, the question that everyone should ask is, did you also feel the presence of the spirit? For in a seance, you are touched by the power of love and those once dead can be seen and heard once more in a uniting of heaven and earth.

Throughout the history of spiritualism those in the spirit world have made remarkable efforts to draw our attention and to open wide the window of belief. It was never meant that we should get stuck in the phenomena or in the message, but to allow ourselves to look beyond to the realisation of the eternal and the real meaning of why they make such attempts to enrich our minds and touch our hearts.

Long before the famous spirit rappings were experienced by the Fox sisters in 1848, the result of which instigated the birth of modern spiritualism and endeavoured to create a comprehension of human intelligence beyond bodily death, in 858 a German Benedictine Monk known as Rudolf of Fulda referred to communications with the spirit world through a series of raps. In fact, the early Catholic church frequently made reference to 'spiritus percutiens' (latin for spirit rapping), but sadly the phenomenon met with disapproval and attempts were enforced to discourage any recognition of efforts by the spirit to commune.

As well as there being an incredible number of physical phenomena in the spiritualist movement, this is also present in the history of Catholic mysticism. The lives of some of the mystics and those who have been recognised and beatified by the Catholic church are full of accounts of spiritual powers that defy known natural law. In nearly every spiritual or religious tradition there are those who have spiritualised themselves through a life of contemplation and devotion, or through acts of selfless love have experienced supernormal powers.

BI-LOCATION

This is a phenomenon where a person is physically transported to another location, and is therefore in more than one place at a time; sometimes these two places can be a great distance apart. This mysterious phenomenon has been documented as being experienced by many people including Parahamansa Yogananda (1893-1952), a yogi and founder of a self-realisation fellowship, Padre Pio (1887- 1968) of Pietrelcina, a Capuchin monk, Carmine Mirabelli and St Faustina.

In many instances, the experience of bi-location has happened spontaneously and, more importantly, when there was a need. It was reported on many occasions that both Padre Pio and St Faustina appeared at the bedsides of people who were either seriously ill or about to pass. It was said of Padre Pio that sometimes it was as though he had begun to fall asleep in the middle of a conversation, or whilst deep in prayer, and his physical body would be quite cold and still; it was on these occasions there would be accounts of him appearing simultaneously at some other distant location.

After the second world war miraculous accounts of Padre Pio appearing to soldiers on the battlefield and saving their lives came flooding into the monastery. There is an incredible account of Padre Pio seen levitating in the air in front of a squadron of American bombers who were under strict instructions to release bombs in order to destroy a munitions dump which was situated very close to the monastery in San Giovanni. On the appearance of Padre Pio, the bombs were mysteriously released early without military intervention, and fell on the intended target; had the bombs been dropped according to given instructions it would have resulted in possible fatalities, but the levitating monk had no doubt enabled many lives to be saved.

The miraculous opens our heart to the mystery of life and to the realisation that the world isn't always as we may have been led to believe. The accounts and tales of extraordinary mediums and other spiritually enlightened souls reveal the hidden depths within man and of the spirit. The quality of our gaze determines the capacity of all that we have the ability to perceive. We should attend to the soul as so much of our life is dedicated to appearances and what we look like outwardly to the world when all the while the inner life beckons us to nourish the spirit. To invest in the spirit is the only guaranteed return we can ever make.

COMMUNICATION OF AN UNLIKELY KIND

The door of possibility is always open and never closed. As in the lives of many other mediums, I have found myself regularly travelling far away from home. I consider myself most richly blessed as, for more years than I would care to tell, I have shared my knowledge of the spirit at spiritualist churches in Vancouver. It is a place I love not just for the spectacular beauty of the snow-capped mountains and the diversity and richness of the landscape, but more importantly the friendship I have found in the warmth of the people there.

Back in 2004 as I was preparing to leave home to go on my annual visit there, I reached for a book I had read many years previously, 'The Autobiography of a Yogi' by Paramhansa Yogananda, as I never ever travel without the companion of a book. As Plato so eloquently said "Books give a soul to the universe, wings to the mind, flight to the imagination and life to everything".

It was on my flight back home that I opened the book with the intention of reading it. Upon doing so I started to feel unsettled. Better, I thought, to try to meditate, so I closed my eyes and focused gently on my breathing, then

118

in my awareness with great clarity I became conscious of the smiling face of Yogananda. Through clairaudience I then began to hear the serenity of his words flowing into my conscious awareness. Yogananda spoke with insight about the evolution of consciousness, the need within the spiritualist movement to pay more attention to spiritualising ourselves with less emphasis on the message, as the message served, to reassure and prove to people of the ultimate truth that we are eternal beings, but what was of the greatest value was effort and devotion to our inner life. I was told unknowingly I had been conveying the essence of the self-realisation fellowship teachings and that I had spent not just one but many lives in India, that the spiritual work that I was doing now was just a continuation of my spiritual agreement to be of service and to help to provide a deeper understanding as to the nature of reality. So much was conveyed that my mind was overwhelmed, and I was buzzing with excitement. Then the doubt began to creep in, what if this is all just a figment of my imagination? Ridiculous as it seems, I found myself apologising to Yogananda and I said, "forgive me but I need to know all I was experiencing was real", but even as I said this, I knew in my soul that it was! To this statement Yogananda replied, "Open the book and you will find much of what I have just spoken to you of will be on the page". This was indeed true for even though I had randomly opened the book the content of the page pertained to much of what had previously been conveyed. My analytical mind was still not convinced, 'ah', I thought, 'but what if this is just a residual memory?', after all, I had read this book some twenty years before.

Inwardly I could hear the voice of Yogananda once more telling me now to open the book one last time and what was on the page would relate to a letter that would be waiting for me on my arrival home. I proceeded to open the book and there staring back at me was a photo of the well-loved Indian Poet Rabindranath Tagore. Little chance of that I thought to myself, but the conversation ended by being told to meditate diligently on 'God conscious-ness' and bring all my focus to the area called the third eye.

The feeling stayed with me as to the reality of my encounter but then, as is always the nature of the rational mind, I began to wonder why such a spiritual being would communicate with me. In the great scheme of things, I was only an ordinary person doing my best to play my part.

On my arrival home I forgot the experience for a moment, until I began to open my mail and came across the familiar handwriting of Eric Hatton. To my amazement I unfolded his letter to discover a photocopy of a letter he had promised to show me on several occasions when I had been staying with him whilst working at his church. The letter he enclosed was written by none other than, yes, you've guessed it, Rabindranath Tagore.

Whilst I had been away, Eric had been clearing out some papers and came across the letter. We had previously shared a conversation on the beauty of Tagore's poetry and Eric had gone to his safe to find this historic letter, that he had in his possession and had been written by Tagore himself, so he could show it to me. It wasn't where he knew he had safely placed it and on each following visit had made many attempts to locate it but had failed to do so. Never forgetting a promise, Eric, true to his word having found the letter, photocopied the original and sent it to me. As if this wasn't enough, he had posted it at about the same time I was actually having the experience and by the time my journey was completed and I had arrived safely home it had reached its destination, just a breath before me. How could I live in denial? I believe it was orchestrated by the spirit in some way to validate the authenticity of my encounter. An experience that has stayed with me and often reminds me that in the universe one life is not any more or less valued than another and, when we are motivated to help people, we to are helped by unseen powers; however likely or unlikely, their support is always there.

Telegram-Adresse
Angleterre, København   7th September 1926.

Dear Mr. Brown,

        Your letter of the 24th August.

        It gives me great joy when I
hear from people telling me how they have been
helped by my works. This appreciation of my
readers is my greatest gratification, and I thank
you very much indeed for having written to me.

        I am sorry that I have not with
me a copy of my 'Letters from Abroad'; but I am
writing to India, and a copy will be sent to
your address.

        Yours sincerely,

        Rabindranath Tagore

MEDIUMS, POETS, AND APPORTS

In the Encyclopaedia of Psychic Science by Nandor Fador, 1934, there are fascinating accounts of the mediumship of Mrs Agnes Guppy. Firstly, she had married into wealth, so there was no underlying need to make a living from her abilities and she was consequently less likely to be subject to any desire to act fraudulently, as a few of her contemporaries may have been. In addition, her seances were often attended by many well-respected people. Secondly, her physical mediumship often occurred in the light, which is helpful in proving the authenticity of proceedings and is exceptional even by today's standards, and in order to prove the apports, which she was commonly known for manifesting.

At times the sitters would be asked their preference as to what they would like to appear. In the presence of Alfred Russell Wallace, the then well-known respected naturalist, fruits of all different types appeared in the order of which they had been asked by those present. Accounts of clay tablets with inscriptions thousands of years old and even a bird's nest, complete with unhatched eggs and a startled bird, once appeared in full view of the sitters. However, the most interesting is the sitting which inspired the American poet Henry Wadsworth Longfellow to write his well know poem 'Psalm of Life" when on a visit to Naples. In a sitting with Mrs Guppy, whilst holding both of her hands, there appeared as if from nowhere not just one but several branches of orange blossom, with a delicate aroma. This experience, in broad daylight, so convinced him of life after death that, after this remarkable phenomenon, he wrote his most well-known poem:

Tell me not in mournful numbers,

Life is but an empty dream,

And the soul is dead that slumbers

122

And things are not what they seem,

Life is real and life is earnest!

And the grave is not its goal

Dust thou art to dust returnest,

Was not spoken of the soul.

My favourite story involving the mediumship of Mrs Guppy is the incredible account of her transportation from her home in Highbury, north London, to the home of Charles Williams, in Lambs Conduit Street. At the time the event occurred, Mrs Guppy had been in her home in the company of a friend, Miss Neyland, doing her accounts and in every sense and meaning of the phrase, minding her own business. However, she was transported to a seance being run by George Williams and Frank Herne, a few miles away. Dressed still in her night clothes and slippers, she landed with a thump in the middle of the seance, much to the astonishment of those attending. Mrs Guppy appeared to be in a trance state, but on becoming conscious was clearly not amused to find herself in the centre of a seance in amongst a group of strangers and all because the spirit, on being asked to bring an apport, had offered that someone present might like to request an article and the reply had, in a joking manner, been to bring Mrs Guppy! Within the space of three minutes the spirit had answered the request and had brought the unexpected medium, followed a short while later by her outdoor clothes and some flowers as an offering.

SYMPHONIES FROM THE SPIRIT.

I felt strongly impressed to include the remarkable story of the mediumship of Rosemary Brown, as in many ways it is incredibly unique and yet I always believed she never really got the credit she so rightly deserved. Unfortunately, I never had the privilege of meeting Rosemary, yet feel incredibly drawn to her as if I have known her in some strange way. Mediumship is more often than not associated with loved ones communicating and proving survival, yet mediumistic powers often function outside the narrow framework of what constitutes proof contained within a message.

The unique mediumship expressed through Rosemary is just that; for she composed in her lifetime over five hundred pieces of music. A virtually impossible accomplishment, considering she had only a rudimentary knowledge of music. The development of her clairaudient abilities meant she could, with ease, hear those iconic composers of the past dictate in musical language new compositions and in some instances unfinished symphonies were completed. Rosemary's abilities were, without any shadow of a doubt, outstandingly remarkable.

With grace and dignity of spirit, in the face of much accusation, sometimes even being classed as being psychologically unstable despite having been subjected to tests which concluded she was of sound mind and an extremely balanced individual, Rosemary quietly went about her life not being deterred by those critical minds who wouldn't even begin to entertain the thought 'what if it is true?'.

Rosemary's first mediumistic encounter with a composer was of the renowned Franz Liszt. She was only seven when she received a communication from him; he chose to tell her in a most simplistic manner that he himself was a composer and a pianist and foretold how one day he would come back and work through her. This prophecy was indeed fulfilled, much later on in Rosemary's life, when a relationship formed where Franz Liszt not only composed his much-loved music through her but co-ordinated a team of other remarkable composers to do the same.

The objective from the spirit team who had been drawn to this challenge was more far reaching then the mere indulgence in their given musical abilities being expressed, it was not just to satisfy their own need but poured from a great love and desire to prove that physical death is a transition from one state of consciousness to another and we will indeed take with us any soul abilities we may possess into the great beyond.

"When man has plumbed the mysterious depth of his veiled consciousness, he will then be able to soar to correspondingly greater heights" the British musical analyst and composer Sir Donald Tovey once dictated from the spirit world, through Rosemary Brown.

In 1969 a BBC documentary was made on the extraordinary abilities of Rosemary it was called 'Mrs Brown and the Composers' (produced by Geoffrey Skelton and Daniel Snowman). During the filming Rosemary was invited to demonstrate her mediumistic abilities. Nervously and under enormous pressure the likes of which she had never known before, she offered an inner request to Liszt, "Be sure you give me something spectacular". There in front of the expectant presence of curious yet sceptical minds, Franz Liszt musically dictated to her the famous 'Grubelei'. A specialist on the works of Liszt, Humphrey Searle stated in support of the proceedings that this was just the sort of piece Liszt would have written in his later years.

Even the legendary composer and conductor Leonard Bernstein invited Rosemary to dine with him at the Savoy; Rosemary's reputation had preceded her, and Bernstein was curious as to how someone with no real musical training could be responsible for such remarkable, musical master-pieces. Keen to find out more about her enigmatic but controversial musical abilities, Bernstein asked Rosemary if she had with her any work to show him. It just so happened that hours before Rosemary had received her invitation to meet him, the spirit team were indeed one step ahead as, that very morning, the Romantic composer Sergei Rachmaninoff communicated and transmitted a new piece of musical genius.

Rosemary frequently questioned, "why me?", as she often felt her musical knowledge was inadequate and had the composers chosen someone else, they may have accomplished more. Liszt was quick to respond and stated "A musical background would have caused you to acquire too many ideas and theories of your own. These would have been an impediment to us".

In an observation as to the nature of mediumship, Rosemary emphasised, like any medium, the importance of subduing the rational mind. How true a statement, as mediumship can be summed up by the medium's ability to get their own self out of the way and surrender to the wonders of the communication.

Although Bernstein was suitably impressed as to the style and quality and proceeded to play the piece by Rachmaninoff and others channelled through Rosemary with great enthusiasm, he couldn't quite go the distance and admit publicly that this indeed was the work of 'so-called dead composers', after all, to do so would be an admission of his belief in mediumship and the reality of life after death and this, of course, would put his reputation on the line; too much was at stake.

Although Rosemary continued to be loyal and dedicated to the spirit it was apparent that those great composers and musical minds felt somewhat disheartened as to the collective response or lack of it, from the general public at large. Rosemary's sudden popularity and her fame, if you can call it that, was short lived and a sense of never having achieved a breakthrough in the way those in the spirit world had intended prevailed. Yet her music lives on and I am sure one day when the world of science declares life after death to be true, Rosemary Brown may then get the true recognition she so rightly deserves, as her team of spirit composers must rank her up there with the best of them. Her dedication to the cause never ever faltered and her faith in the world unseen never tired.

REMARKABLE POWERS

Over the passing of the years, I have been incredibly privileged to either witness remarkable mediumistic powers or be in the company of those who shared their lives with either friends or family who were physical mediums. Some stories touch you profoundly and, if my memory serves me well, I first heard the following story way back in the 1980's told by the very humble Tom Harrison, the son of the extraordinary physical medium Minnie Harrison. The following is an extract from one of his books 'Visits by Our Friends from the Other Side' - I like this story so much because it reveals the love the spirit world has for us still and how there was a desire to give a gift as an expression of thanks to honour Minnie's birthday!

One of the most unusual and certainly the largest apport received through my mother's mediumship occurred not in a home circle sitting, but in my mother's home on her 53rd birthday, 17th March 1948. Mam and Dad had a kitchen with a small walk-in type of pantry with no window only a zinc gauze vent. I lived about ten minutes' drive from them and about four o'clock our telephone rang. It was Mam asking if I could go straight there as there was something unusual she wanted me to see.

When I arrived Mam and Dad were sitting in the kitchen having a cup of tea. Mam usually had a smile on her face, but on this occasion it seemed rather enigmatic. She realised I was keen to see what she had telephoned about and immediately said "just open the pantry door, son, but be very careful". Naturally I was very curious and a little apprehensive but did exactly as I was asked. I opened it very slowly but because of the lack of light saw nothing unusual for a moment or two. Then as I opened it wider to step inside I was halted in my tracks!

There at my feet on the floor of the pantry was a mass of lilac blossom filling the whole floor space and as high as the first shelf, about three feet high! I turned and looked at Mam who, with an even bigger grin said, "I thought you would be surprised", an understatement if ever there was. But the explanation was even more surprising. Mam had made the customary pot of tea in the afternoon, got the milk jug out of the pantry, closed the door behind her and sat on her chair adjacent to the door. She then realised that she had forgotten the sugar, turned on her chair and opened the door again, to be confronted by this amazing sight on the pantry floor. One moment earlier, when she got the milk, the floor had been absolutely clear. Now it was packed with lilac blossom. Naturally they were both dumbfounded and Mam's first thought was to ring me. I was as amazed as they were. Instinctively I knew it was not a practical joke. Mam and Dad didn't do those things and Mam wouldn't bring me back to the shop 'on a fool's errand'.

Come the following Saturday evening circle, Aunt Agg again pre-empted our question by asking us to tell our Min, as she always called my Mother, that they had been delighted to be able to bring

128

her such a special birthday gift from Germany spirit friends who were
so close to her! The darkness of the pantry had afforded the ideal
conditions and it was another example of Mam's mediumship. But
for a change, this time she had been the first to witness it!

A dear friend and colleague Glyn Edwards had the privilege in his early days
of his mediumistic development, to take part regularly in a seance with a
local physical medium. During one particular seance every person present
received an 'apport' from the spirit world of a coin, remarkably the date on
each coin was the year of each person's birth. The implications are incredible. Firstly, it means the spirit had the knowledge of the year everyone was
born, which is amazing in itself, but, secondly, they somehow managed to
gather a specific coin with the appropriate date on and make it manifest in
the room in front of the correct person.

Glyn also loved to tell the story of a piano which was in another part of the
room away from where everyone was seated for seance proceedings and
hadn't been touched by anyone present. Following a lot of excitable conversation with the spirit, through the power of the medium and co-operation of
the spirit, the piano rose in the air and levitated above the heads of those
present. Glyn stated that it was not a good time to doubt the reality of the
spirit world as 'just think of the consequences of a heavy piano swaying in
time to the singing, just a few feet above your head'!

IN THE FOOTSTEPS OF SAINT FRANCIS

Back in 2015 a close friend Ilse, from the Netherlands, organised a short
break to Italy. I had for a long time wanted to visit Assisi, the birthplace of
St Francis, but had never quite managed to organise a break and this was
taken out of my hands and with the sort of kindness only a good friend
would show, as Ilse had arranged it all for me. On the penultimate day of

the holiday, we were visiting the Basilica in Assisi. As is the norm for this particular time of year, it was filled with tourists. Now If you have ever been to Italy you will most definitely know that any mealtime is an important event! So, as lunchtime approached the Basilica began to empty, so much so that it went within a few moments from being extremely busy to, with the exception of a few wardens, nearly empty. Almost spontaneously, Ilse and I both decided to take advantage of the situation and sitting down in the pews close to the tomb of St Francis, began to quietly meditate and soak in the intense energy. At that time two very good friends were seriously ill and so I thought that, as I was in such a sacred place, I would begin by first of all sending out healing prayers. Being in a beautiful setting, imbued with the power of the spirit and dedicated to not only St Francis but in some instances Padre Pio, I thought I might direct my prayers to these extraordinary souls.

Within a few short moments of sitting, an overwhelming fragrance of very distinctive roses manifested, not only could I smell the divine aroma but as I opened my eyes in excitement and tapped my friend gently on the arm, before I could utter a word Ilse said to me, "I know, I can smell it too". Padre Pio is known for the smell of roses that manifested from the stigmata that he bore after his visitation from Jesus; for fifty years the wounds would bleed but they released the fragrance of the sweetest rose perfume. Needless to say, it was a shared experience from the spirit world; I believe partly in acknowledgment of the healing prayers being sent but also a reflection of the fact that the two sick people were both very special teachers in their own right. It was as though the other world were saying that they were held within the grace of love.

The following day we both retraced the footsteps we had previously taken and sat in exactly the same place at the same time, just to satisfy the voice of logic that so frequently makes you question after you have experienced

130

something of such a nature, but also to be sure it wasn't an air-freshener placed in an out of the way position that randomly released a fragrance but nothing, absolutely nothing.

Over the years I have received a number of 'apports' from the spirit world, both in a seance environment and at other times when I have been in need of reassurance from the spirit world that I was not alone in all that was troubling me at the time. I have found the manifestation of such gifts never random but always extremely evidential. Once when I was feeling a sense of hopelessness and despondency, sitting in my living room on the floor leaning against my sofa, I felt as if something had dropped beside me with a little clink of sound and when I looked, there right beside my arm was my father's Atlantic star medal he had received after the war in recognition for his efforts. Now, a star has particular meaning between myself and my father and his medal had previously been in a wardrobe in a large click-sealed container within a smaller jewellery box; no-one else was present in the house at the time.

On another occasion, I had been visiting the crematorium where my father's ashes had been scattered. I had never actually been here at the anniversary of his passing since I had moved from the south of England to Scotland. However, my sister and I decided to make a visit there and our first call was to the small room that held the book of remembrance in a rather large glass case.

Reading what had been entered into the book at the time of his passing moved me greatly, despite the long years that had gone past, as I recalled the vivid emotions. The room was sparse and included the glass case as mentioned, a book on a small table to write down any tributes and a very inappropriate sign saying in bold lettering 'no flowers in here please'.

My sister suggested I should share a few thoughts in the little book, which I did, and on turning back around towards the glass case once more, noticed a pale pink carnation placed slap-bang in the middle, blocking our view of what previously could clearly be seen. Heaven knows what possessed me to say what I did next, for as I picked up the flower I said to our father "if you were going to give a gift then you should have given us two flowers, as we live 600 miles apart". Within that very same moment my sister caught sight of another flower, just at the side of the glass case and directly below the sign that stated 'no flowers', this carnation was much darker then the first and a deep fuchsia pink.

Our minds raced in a very logical manner, questioning if the flowers could in any way have been there before, but we just hadn't noticed. Possibly, if you feel inclined to think in a very logical manner, the flower that was at the side may well have been missed, but most definitely not the pale pink one placed in such a strategic position. In addition, I must add that our Dad had a cheeky sense of humour and at times could be a bit of a non-conformist, so I think he would rather have enjoyed the fact that, from his side of life, rules such as 'no flowers in here please' might just not apply!

On leaving we had to pass through a walkway where people could leave flowers in memory of those they loved, the vases hung elegantly on a wall, creating a blaze of colour filled with all types of flowers which seemed to be imbued with the fragrance of both deep grief and love. There I noticed, a little apart, one container with the pale pink carnation on the top row and another with the darker carnation on the bottom row. As if signifying the distance between the locations of where we both lived, were the two different varieties of carnation.

It was a Sunday morning and as my sister drove us both along the driveway through the grounds, suddenly a stream of cars full of people appeared.

If they had arrived 30 minutes earlier maybe the energy would not have been so conducive for the spirit world to transport flowers as an act of love.

BUTTERFLIES FROM HEAVEN

An apport of a delicate filigree butterfly brooch once materialised at a seance that I was present at, with the medium Scott Milligan. It manifested in strict conditions where the medium had been thoroughly searched; Scott has always been incredibly thorough, always insisting that he be searched to the satisfaction of those present. Interestingly, I had once owned exactly the same brooch, when I was younger. I had bought it when on a holiday in Yugoslavia, as a memento of my very first holiday abroad. The spirit people have often said an apport is normally an article which has been lost or unloved in some way. Needless to say, I had lost the brooch a short while after having bought it, and I found the re-appearance of the exact same one many years later extremely thought-provoking; had the spirit world taken it only to return it again at a future date, when it would have emotional significance? We little comprehend, with their greater vision, the enormous lengths those in the spirit go to in reminding us of their constant love. They must have an awareness in some way that a future opportunity will present itself to bring the extraordinary gift of both comfort and proof. For the timing was impeccable, as it occurred just a few weeks after a very dear friend, Heather Hatton, had passed to the spirit world and butterflies were incredibly evidential and had a specific meaning to her.

Just a few weeks after, I was the course organiser on a week at the Arthur Findlay College and Jose Medrado, the Brazilian medium and founder of the City of light Institute, an organisation that provides support and welfare needs to thousands of needy children and families in Salvador, was doing a demonstration of mediumistic Trance Painting when before our very eyes a butterfly flew out of a painting. I must add two points of interest; the first being that when he was younger, Medrado had been a physical medium and was known to materialise the full form of a spirit person in red light, secondly that the butterfly was the same colour as the painting. This was witnessed by everyone present and followed on from the butterfly brooch apport at the seance just two weeks before, but this time Minister Eric Hatton was present and I'm sure you have made the connection that Eric was married to Heather. The intelligence of the spirit communicators is such that not only was the butterfly conveying its own message but, additionally, the year before at another demonstration by Medrado, a friend had bought a particular painting for Eric and Heather to celebrate their golden wedding anniversary and it just happened to be with perfect synchronicity, that the same spirit artist had also been working through Medrado at that time. Dear Eric was still in the early stages of bereavement and yet here was remarkable reassurance from the spirit world of a love that is eternal and unchanged by death. For the butterfly flew out of the painting and even though was a substantially large room, danced in flight around Eric a few times, then past the other tutors before making its way to the window.

Eric, having had extensive experience of sitting with some of the most remarkable mediums in the history of Spiritualism, including physical mediums of the calibre of Alec Harris, suggested that everyone who witnessed the manifestation should testify to what was experienced, as the nature of the mind is such that, after the event, it will invariably try to rationalise the proceedings in some way to provide a more logical explanation.

An experience such as this lingers in your memory. Many, but thankfully not all, of these remarkable people have passed know. Life can be strange; one day you are sharing a moment with someone, creating a memory and you turn around and they too have passed silently into the great beyond. Ultimately, we will all find out the reality of the spirit world one day for ourselves, for death is the one certainty that life brings.

Yet we are the richer for having known such people and are changed because of the love we have shared and the great truths that have been realised through all we have encountered. As the poet Alfred Lord Tennyson said, "O for the touch of a vanished hand, And the sound of a voice that is still". Inner longing with the co-operation of the spirit and the presence of a very accomplished physical medium, can indeed become a reality. A dear friend, through the mediumship of Gordon Higginson, was able to experience the joy of seeing his father materialise and walk out of a cabinet in the natural glow of moonlight softly streaming in through the window. His father not only fully materialised but walked across the room, clasped his son's face and spoke to him. When I asked him what it was like he replied, "it was like touching heaven". How often those who have been bereaved have stated they would give anything just to feel once more the touch of their loved one's hands, or to hold them again. Isn't it all just an absolute miracle?

You may be thinking where have these past abilities and powers gone? I personally don't think they have gone anywhere and are still present in the young today, it's just that we need to devote more time to development and to learn not to give up when nothing appears to be happening. We can never know, or indeed tell, when that moment may occur when the unseen may manifest and become seen. Maybe the need from the spirit is not so great now and in we may have outgrown the need to receive proof in such a manner. Possibly we have moved from the age of 'seeing is believing' to 'believing is seeing', as there has indeed been an enormous shift in the thinking of mankind. Communication is now taking more current forms of expression, but without doubt I am sure the abilities are still there. However, just as anything worthwhile needs a little patience and dedication, there is so much in the way of expectations being put on us all now and the demands of life are great, maybe we all need to step away from the fast pace of life in order to rekindle the light within, so the voice of the spirit may be heard.

Some people may think why invest so much of your time and energy with the dead, you need to be fully present in life, but that's the very point, spirit is life, life eternal; the knowledge of which enriches the quality of our living here.

A great deal of physical mediumship takes place in closed circles now as it did in years gone by. Like all forms of mediumship, physical mediumship needs to be treated with great reverence and respect, as hostile environments are not conducive to any type of mediumship reaching its potential. Understandably those who are presently experiencing the phenomena of the spirit are extremely protective of their abilities. It has been the case in the past that physical mediumship was taken out into areas where the abilities of the medium could be subjected to the harsh opinions of sceptical minds and the voice of the critics too soon. Any inherent abilities need trust and patience to develop properly and should be established enough to withstand varying atmospheres. For mediumship is truly a creative power and, as anyone from the world of creative expression will know, needs the right atmosphere to be nurtured into fullness of being. It is love that should be a first port of call when considering developing latent mediumistic powers, love and only love.

No true medium can work without the presence and help of the spirit and behind every achievement, however great or small, are the unseen hands of the invisible. We are the richer for their presence and more deeply blessed then we could ever know, and it is important never to forget this.

References:

Visits by Our Friends From 'The Otherside' by T. Harrison, SNPP

Unfinished Symphonies by Rosemary Brown, Corgi

Saint Padre Pio, Man of Hope by Renzo Allegri, Servant Books

Alec Harris, The full story of his mediumship; by Louie Harris, SNPP

Encyclopedia of Psychic Science: by Nandor Fodor, Arthur's Press 1933

Further reading:

Life after death: living Proof by T. Harrison, SNPP

Autobiography of a Yogi by Paramhansa Yoganada,
Self Realisation Fellowship Publishers

Leslie Flint Voices in the Dark, Psychic Book Club Publishing

MEDIUMSHIP TOUCHING THE STARS

CHAPTER SEVEN

PRACTICAL SUGGESTIONS

"And the day came,

When the risk to remain tight in a bud

Was more painful than

The risk it took to bloom"

Anais Nin

CULTIVATING AN INNER RECEPTIVITY

The following suggestions are designed to awaken and enhance mediumistic powers of awareness. If practised everyday they will gently encourage the natural growth and expression of these innate heightened states of spiritual awareness. By openness of mind, we allow ourselves to explore the realms of possibility.

It is paramount that you, first of all, feel comfortable with who you are as a spiritual being. Despite all the opinions and judgements you may have made about yourself in the past, recognise that you are perfect right here and now and you are just the way you are supposed to be.

Preparation of spirit, body and mind is crucial. You can't experience what you don't believe, so cultivating a belief in your own capabilities, in your true nature, is essential. You cannot know the power within you if you keep telling yourself you are not good enough; we really can't expect people, or indeed the spirit, to give us something we do not feel worthy of receiving. It is as though we collectively go round in a trance of unworthiness and then wonder why what we inwardly desire never manifests. All those great souls who have accomplished their dreams didn't always have an easy life but were guided by an impetus to make a difference and realised they were much more than the limiting circumstances of the past, that so often many people encounter. Additionally, if in your thinking you continually identify with your mind you will experience the limitation of the mind, if you identify with your spirit you will become one with the spirit and experience freedom.

CONFIDENCE

'I am filled with life divine,

Therefore boundless good is mine'.

Affirmation

I have often used the above little affirmation It is easy to remember as there is a gentle rhythm contained within it and, simple though it is, it can be extremely helpful in eradicating negative opinions we may have got into the habit of having about ourselves. Invite into your life the possibility of everything nourishing and beautiful.

Confidence is vital so allow yourself to feel confident, this is easier if you accept yourself and realise you don't have to do anything other than be who you are, to acknowledge that you are enough. Everyone is a work in progress and to expect to be perfect is too great a burden, instead aspire to perfect your capacity to love.

Allow the statement 'I am confident' to move through your mind for a moment - repeat this statement as frequently as you can. How does it make you feel, or change the way you perceive yourself?

Identify 'where' within you experience the feeling of being confident.

Now, with your intent, ask the spirit to give you a colour which you can associate with the feeling of confidence; you may perceive this in different ways, you could feel the colour or see it in your mind's eye, or even be bathed inwardly in a particular hue. Notice how this colour makes you feel. It may be a colour you would least expect; this is always a good indication that you have received it naturally. Continue to allow the experience to come to you, don't create or coerce it. If you try too hard it won't happen in the same way. Instead, just remain receptive. Once you have experienced something, rest in the awareness of this moment and whatever you received know it is real.

Recall a time in your life when you achieved something you had been working hard to attain or a time in life when you were glowing with happiness because of a blessing received. Locate your attention in how this made you feel at the same time feel an awareness of the colour you experienced earlier, absorb the memory and the feelings associated with this memory, of happiness merging with the colour blending together as one.

Lastly, inwardly visualise the image of someone who has always been a source of inspiration to you, recall their facial expressions with as much detail as possible. Once you have done this bring all three experiences together.

141

The colour you personally associate now with confidence, the memory of the feeling of happiness and the visual image of the person who has been a source of inspiration.

From now on use this as an inward reminder to always begin with placing your focus on the colour. If you do this often enough, confidence will begin to grow and become an integral part of who you are. For the colour now embodies all the positive qualities which will overcome any doubt. This will enable you to always begin in a positive way. By taking your mind back to this moment, the association that you now have with confidence will fill your awareness. Remember energy flows where attention goes.

ATTUNING TO THE SPIRIT

Now the next step is to begin with attuning yourself to the spirit. So, ensure you are sitting comfortably.

- *Begin by relaxing your physical self, you can do this just by directing this thought to your body.*

- *Become aware of the quiet movement of your breath and each beat of your heart.*

- *Feel a gentle softening within each breath and a relaxing of your physical body as you let go of all the stress and strain that so often you carry within*

- *Notice a sense of peace which gently seems to replace the tension.*

- *Be the observer as you start to pay attention to the natural rhythm of your breath.*

- *Now with your intent expand your awareness, reach out with the power within you to the atmosphere within the room you are sitting in, feel it*

142

and experience it using your sensitivity.

- *How does it speak to you, for everything in the universe is energy?*

- *Next allow an expansion of the power within you, the power of your own spiritual awareness, the love that you are.*

- *Become one with this feeling until you begin to lose any awareness of self.*

- *Just stay held within the experience of love and being loved. If the mind begins to become distracted, don't feed it or pay any attention. Simply allow any thought that comes and goes to pass-by, you are not your thoughts.*

- *Be where your awareness arises, be present within this space.*

- *Notice how in this state of peacefulness you feel a part of all life, in fact you are life for the totality of existence is in you.*

- *Now just rest for a while held within the grace of a limitless love and divine power.*

PERCEIVING THE SPIRIT

Now that you have become peaceful and created an inner stillness, receptivity to the presence of the spirit is possible.

- *First, set the intent.*

- *Second, believe it is possible.*

- *Third, become receptive to the spirit.*

- *When communicating with the spirit it is essential that the mind is free*

143

from distraction and desire.

• *Remove all expectations of how you think the communication should be and any tendencies you may have to judge.*

• *Allow yourself to become at one with the spirit, inviting those in the unseen world to be present within your field of awareness.*

You may experience the communication in many ways. Through the language of feeling, the power of inner seeing or the experience of hearing or simply knowing. One is not any better than the other, they are just different and to start with the spirit will use the faculty that is strongest within you.

CLAIRCOGNIZANCE

Claircognizance, is possibly the least definable of all ways of experiencing the communication. Yet at the same time can be extremely powerful and accurate. Information received in this manner simply means there is no opportunity for involvement of the mind, which increases the likelihood of the evidence being exact. The experience of knowing arises as if from deep within, almost without an awareness of what is coming next. It is as though the medium is swept along by a flow of communication and without any effort becomes immersed in the process. Once this has happened, all now that is required is to maintain the energy of trust and belief in both the spirit and yourself as a channel.

Individual development should always be progressive and depends upon a willingness and receptivity to be open to continually explore new ways of receiving the communication. Mediumship is constantly reforming itself and the spirit world keen to experiment different ways to convey the message.

Before you begin to communicate try speaking mentally to those in the spirit, suggest that they allow you to see their handwriting, what does it reveal

144

about who they were? Or invite the opportunity to convey something which has emotional significance. Anything which enables you, as a sensitive, to move beyond the boundaries so often created by your own doubts and limits.

Refrain from trying during the process of receiving the communication, offer to the spirit before you start, then surrender to the universe and see what gently touches your perception, so the information arises readily in your awareness.

CLAIRSENTIENCE

For the following exercises you will need someone to practise with.

We are sentient beings and our feelings shape our experience of reality, but also feeling is the language of the spirit.

* *So gently set the intent begin to bring your focus to the area we call the solar plexus.*

* *Next pay attention to any feelings which were not there a moment ago.*

* *Identify 'where' within you experience this.*

* *Begin to observe and notice, but without effort or trying too hard.*

* *Become aware of nothing other than what you sense.*

* *Who is there, get to know the spirit person, just as you would with anyone new. If you meet someone for the first time you make an effort to get to know who they are, not by bombarding them with a multitude of questions but allowing them the opportunity to share what they wish to convey. Why should it be any different with those in the spirit world.*

* *Allow the story of who they are to gently unfold, don't interpret or try*

to understand. If you do this, you will bring in your analytical mind and this will be a source of distraction.

* *It may be as subtle as a gentle knowing; if this is so, explore the experience.*

AWAKENING CLAIRVOYANT ABILITIES

Now try to experiment with the possibility of inner seeing.

* *Once more set the intent.*

* *Gently allow yourself to become receptive.*

* *Fix your gaze on a focal point, just in front of you and slightly up to the right. Doing this can enhance concentration.*

* *If you feel your eyelids naturally want to close allow them to, but not for too long, when you begin this is alright, but if you remain with your eyes closed for too long it will disable rather enable, as you are more likely to start concentrating too hard which will activate the analytical mind. Bring your awareness to the centre of your forehead, a focal point associated with inner vision, on the screen of your consciousness are you aware of an image? If so, allow this to happen of its own volition, so the image is happening naturally rather than you trying to create it yourself.*

* *If it is a spirit person describe who you see, or if it is an object allow yourself to become aware of its significance in relation to the spirit communicator.*

* *Stay with the experience not allowing yourself to become distracted. Continue to give as much information as you can.*

DEVELOPING CLAIRAUDIENCE

- *Again set the intent.*

- *This time bring your focus and awareness to the experience of inner listening.*

- *Pay attention to the natural rhythm of the breath, until it begins to align your focus.*

- *Now this time with the next inward breath you are listening.*

- *As you breathe out you are expanding.*

- *Notice any sounds within your own body, you may hear the beat of your heart or the sound the breath makes as you breathe in and out.*

- *Continue - as you breathe in you are listening and as you breathe out you are expanding.*

- *This time inviting the possibility to begin to hear sounds not normally audible to the physical ear, beyond your normal range of hearing.*

- *If you become aware of a sound allow it to take you on the journey of who is there in the spirit. You may perceive a name, a song, or sounds associated with the communicator's place of work, or even the voice of the spirit person speaking to you. There are many ways in which they can impart information which allow you to know who they are and the story of their life to unfold.*

Whatever you do don't doubt or deny, instead be open and receptive to the presence of the spirit and the multitude of ways in which they communicate.

Value being in the presence of the spirit and to experience the joy and

147

wonder of communicating, it shouldn't ever become a chore. The more relaxed you are the easier it will become, for both yourself and those in the spirit world. If you try too hard energetically it will negate the efforts of those who are attempting to communicate.

ALWAYS REMEMBER

• Positive belief: Empowers

• Fear and doubt: Dis-empowers

• Confidence: Life enhancing

• Lack of confidence: Life denying.

Celebrate each communication as an achievement and take one step at a time. If you are dedicated, it will in time be within your capacity to give a fluent communication which is understood. Never forget to give thanks to those in the unseen world, for their journey is one of love and their efforts to touch this level once more are great.

HELPFUL HINTS FOR DEVELOPING CLAIRAUDIENCE

• The vibration of sound can be felt through your entire being, as there exist so many ways to really hear. This explains how some profoundly deaf musicians and composers can still perform, as the experience of hearing is not always located in the ear.

• During the process of clairaudience, it izzs true to say that sometimes there is not an actual 'sound', but rather impressions perceived using your spiritual senses.

• If you begin to listen consciously, your perception of sound will heighten.

• You can feel a sound, the vibration of which can be felt through your

148

solar plexus and even through the tips of your fingers or throat. Many mediums have experienced sounds from the spirit in varying ways.

- Practise listening to the tone of a person's voice, allow yourself to feel the vibration by moving your awareness beyond the sound. What does the voice reveal about who they really are, beyond the persona that is portrayed? I have often given students the task to read a person by the vibration of their voice, this encourages a deepening connection with sound. The American poet Longfellow said the soul reveals itself through the voice. How true this is, for sometimes as you engage in listening to someone speak their voice soothes the soul, but by contrast there are those whose voices can feel discordant and in their company you feel unsettled. Surely this is a natural response and indicator as to whether you are in harmony with a person. For the voice carries the intention of our heart and to the one who truly listens, the deepest self may be revealed.

- The more you set the intent and begin to truly listen, the more you will begin to hear.

- Experiment with ways of inner listening. Bring your awareness and attention to the space between each sound. This naturally encourages our capacity to encounter sound on a deeper, richer level and prepares for the possibility to perceive with our spiritual senses, expanding the potential for communication.

- Extend your intention of hearing, stretching as far as you can. By bringing your attention to allowing yourself to hear in an extended manner, it will encourage the activation of any dormant clairaudient abilities.

- Experiment by offering the intent to hear in as many ways as possible, different sounds from the spirit world. Can you hear the tonal quality of

149

the spirit person's voice, or sounds associated with their profession? Alternatively, sounds within their home - maybe the communicator liked to listen to the radio. There is so much information that can be received through the power of hearing, but we must first train ourselves to be still and take our attention to the possibility of what we can hear.

If you are dedicated and devote time and energy, before long you will be perceiving the spirit communicators as fluently and clearly as having a conversation with someone here.

In the history of spiritualism there have been some remarkable mediums who could hear the spirit with such clarity that it was as though the spirit person was physically present within the room. It was the norm not only to convey the spirit person's essence, but to give first names, surnames, rank and position when in the forces, and their address. Some of the outstanding mediums working at this level were Estelle Roberts, Helen Hughes and Gordon Higginson. However, there were many more and it was no coincidence that our finest exponents of spiritualism demonstrated their unique abilities when the world was in great need, particularly during the second world war. It was indeed spiritualism's finest hour, when extensive loss was at its greatest and from the shores of eternity the voice of the spirit brought comfort to the bereaved and renewed man's hope in the glorious truth that there is no death. The sun goes down but to rise on some fairer shore.

During a time of intense sitting to be at one with the spirit, I asked the spirit world, "Why, in our present time, doesn't there seem to be the same prevalence of clairaudient mediums, in comparison with bygone days?". The spirit responded by suggesting in our current time we are suffering from saturation of sound and have consequently desensitised ourselves collectively to vibrations from other realities. Even in a conversation with another, the biggest communication problem is we don't listen to understand, we listen to reply. Yet the answer lies in retraining our focus and attention in the art of inner listening, so that we may awaken the faculty to truly hear. What a gift it is to truly listen and, in listening, to really hear.

THE LANGUAGE OF SPIRIT SHORTHAND

In all the years of working with the spirit world it has never ceased to amaze me just how intelligent those who communicate are and, even though it is required of the medium to simply be the conduit, it has become evident how the spirit communicator will draw upon the medium's life experiences, memories of people known and places visited. In fact, anything they know the medium has an understanding of that they can use to get the message across, before the opportunity has passed. Never underestimate just how resourceful the spirit can be, they clearly have an awareness of how important it is to convey as much meaningful information as possible, in the easiest way available. Hence the expression I use, the 'language of shorthand'.

When you have an opportunity to practise your mediumistic abilities on someone, it's always best to have someone you know very little about, especially regarding those in the spirit world. It's a little like an artist always needs a blank canvas to start a painting and, importantly, it helps you discern what is actually coming from the spirit world, instead of the information you already know and thus enables confidence to grow.

Begin by allowing your attention to move to the offering 'who has the person in front of you brought with them from the spirit world'? Who loves and cares for them enough to want to communicate? Then begin to listen with the totality of your awareness as there are so many ways of which the spirit will communicate. Every piece of information is as a brush stroke on the canvas which will give life to your communicator until the whole picture has been painted and a satisfying glow of recognition lights up the recipient's face. Remember at this point never to judge the information as it moves through your awareness.

I will never forget giving a sitting to a lady whose son had passed in his late teens. Such a young life with so much potential to give. At the end of the communication, after having identified himself, he said, "Mum, it's not the length of your years that matters, your age is just a number, what matters is that in your life you have known love, that's what counts". How moving. Sometimes you can't help but be deeply touched by all that takes place in the process of communicating and I could only hope that in some small way his words had eased her heartache, for in his own life he had known love in the support of his mother, who loved him more than life itself. We are the richer for having loved.

INSPIRED AND AUTOMATIC WRITING

"But words are things and a small drop of ink,

Falling like dew, upon a thought,

Produces that which makes thousands,

Perhaps millions think"

Lord Byron.

The beauty of both inspired and automatic writing is that you don't have to travel anywhere or even meet up with other people to develop it, it is simply between you and the spirit world and can be explored in the comfort of your own home. The result of which can ultimately lead to a deeper blending with those in the unseen world and allows an opportunity for timeless wisdom to be expressed.

There exists a notable difference between inspiration and automatic writing, with practice one may merge gracefully into the other. Inspiration noticeably differs from writing from our everyday awareness, although many writers describe an experience of being moved by a flow of inspiration as if they are aware of the words flowing to them, so there are places where one merges with the other. It is essential not to get caught in the trap of wanting to label everything, but to adopt an attitude of mind that is flexible and at ease removed from a need to be result-orientated.

INSPIRATION

Inspiration can be compared to a flame within; we have to first connect with feeling for it to be ignited, in order to be real, authentic and alive to the moment. Words have no life force if feeling is absent. If you are invited to speak or write inspirationally the mind should first be free in order to be able to move into the experience of true inspiration.

It is helpful to allow a word or image of something beautiful to be a source of inspiration. Adopting a meditative or contemplative state of mind may help or try sitting in the power and invite the spirit world to be present and influence you. When we begin from a place of deeper blending and connection, our capacity to be inspired is enhanced. So often everyday things are frequently taken for granted but can be experienced in a new way; it's as though by engaging the totality of our focus we facilitate a richer connection. Try holding the image or word in your mind and allow yourself to become one with it, then see what thoughts and feelings arise and begin to write them down. Try not to make a judgment but allow the movement or rhythm to flow through you.

153

Before you begin to speak, pause first and take a centering breath. It helps, if you imagine the power of your spirit filling the entire room you are in, this generates a feeling of expansion and a sense of greater connectiveness. Spontaneity breathes life into the spoken word and enables the speaker to blend with the power of the spirit, as the energy is freer. Rehearsing or comparing what you have to say, will only locate your attention in your head. When you are free from the need to prepare or compare, the analytical mind is less inclined to interfere. This creates an inner receptivity, enabling the speaker to be truly inspired and meet both the individual and collective needs of each person present and touch souls!

Always remember, if you pause for a moment, don't panic, instead be aware that this creates emphasis and acts like punctuation, allowing space for new thought to flow.

Sir George Trevelyan believed in what he described as the 'doctrine of the living word' which implied never using notes. He said, "If one needs to look at a bit of paper to find out what they think then the thoughts are not of burning significance". The challenge he believed is to speak the living word, that starts a flow of inspiration and is audible to everyone in the room. By audible, he meant the language of feeling and energy which was expressed within every word.

All people have a need to express something, to add to life. To be a motiva-tional or inspired speaker, you can inspire others to discover for themselves. When you speak from the heart in such a way you have the capacity to touch the heart's divine centre which is eternal. Yet a flame must be nourished by a spiritual practice of some kind, otherwise life can harden us and make us forget our true nature. To strive for a balance always between the head and the heart, activity and stillness, to nourish the body as well as the mind, will help provide the harmony required to progress.

154

AUTOMATIC WRITING.

Automatic writing is best described as a form of writing which is produced entirely involuntarily, when the person's attention is focused elsewhere, the medium has no awareness of the topic of writing as it merely passes through their hand. Historically, tremendous speeds would be witnessed, and the style of handwriting would be completely different from the medium's own more familiar style. The subjects varied from philosophy to details of life in the spirit world and even languages not known by the medium. This phenomenon can occur when the medium is in a conscious waking state or in a passive altered state, both are normal, and it arises from a medium's ability to blend and surrender to the influence of the spirit. With automatic writing, the information is not filtered through the consciousness of the medium and has the advantage of not being influenced by the thoughts and opinions of the medium.

This form of mediumship became significantly popular in the late nineteenth and early twentieth centuries, as it was much quicker and considerably more effective than communicating through the knocks and raps associated with the birth of modern spiritualism. The elevation of objects and levitation of tables which often swayed in time to the singing of those gathered, or table tilting where a table would move in sequence to letters of the alphabet, tapping out messages, although better than nothing at all proved to be a slow, laborious way of communicating. The spirit world, keen to explore the newly discovered attention of those here on earth, with great swiftness moved on to a less strenuous type of communicating where they could get the message across without too much in the way of extraneous effort.

Automatists sprung up everywhere, like wildflowers at the beginning of spring, and soon replaced the earlier ways. Initially a planchette was used, this was a specially designed board where a pen was attached enabling the

155

hand of the medium to just gently touch the surface of the board, thus helping to prevent the medium from being able to direct or coerce the communication. This method however proved to be restricting as the writing was not always easy to decipher, so mediums soon adopted the practice of lightly holding the pen in their hands and inviting the presence of the spirit to use them as a channel. Esteemed mediums such as William Stainton Moses, William Stead and Leanora Piper all experienced this form of mediumship.

The automatist Geraldine Cummings described the phenomena beautifully as "a form of writing where the pen appears to direct the writer instead of the writer directing the pen". Which is why she preferred to call the experience 'spirit writing'. Her book 'The Road to Immortality' gives an interesting account of life in the spirit world.

Spiritist medium Chico Xavier, 1910-2002, who followed the Spiritist doctrine founded by Allan Kardec, had the most remarkable gift, motivated by a deep desire to ease the suffering of others. He would devote two evenings a week, through an ability that was called 'psychography', to channeling writing letters from the spirit world for those who eagerly gathered to see him and receive a communication from their loved ones. The letters written through his extraordinary mediumship always provided not only the gift of comfort to those that were fortunate enough to receive them, but evidence stating facts and details only known to family members. During the course of his lifetime, he was the channel for 496 books, which included a wide and diverse range of topics far beyond his everyday knowledge, in addition to thousands of spirit communications through the form of a letter. Xavier was responsible for popularising Spiritism in Brazil which now has over five million followers.

Carlos Mirabelli, also from Brazil, both spoke and wrote under the influence of the spirit in foreign languages. Whatever the nature of the topic or however complex the nature of the subject, the spirit could fluently and without hesitation for breath, speak rapidly in over thirty languages, languages not known to the medium himself in everyday waking consciousness. His mediumship was considered both mind-expanding and breath-taking.

It seems to be apparent that the type of mediumship demonstrated by the mediums who have been born in Brazil is of a very powerful nature, whether this is partly to do with the naturalness of the medium's abilities, in addition to inherent powers that haven't been over-schooled, is a point worth considering. Of course, education is of immense value but only if it is not to the detriment of the natural abilities latent within the medium, that can become stifled and manufactured. Brazil in the past has been a predominately Catholic orientated country and consequently has led to a great depth of reverence and respect being cultivated in the hearts and minds of the people. I often reflect that our first mediums were taught by those in the spirit world; maybe a return to acquiring the art of paying attention to those who know more might be conducive to raising the standards in our present day.

SUGGESTIONS TO HELP INVITE THE POSSIBILITY OF INSPIRED OR AUTOMATIC WRITING.

- *First, sit in a place where you know you will not be disturbed.*

- *It may help to play some music, whatever inspires you most.*

- *Try repeatedly drawing the figure eight as this helps disarm the rational mind. Like a zero, the number flows back into itself and represents eternity and gently facilitates the integration of the right and left hemispheres of the brain. Writing your name backwards or even scribbling will have the same effect and the movement is helpful.*

- *Pay attention to your breath, allowing the gentle rhythm of breathing to create a feeling of inner calm.*

- *Offer your intent to the spirit world.*

- *Invite the presence of the spirit to use you as a channel.*

- *Hold the pen without too much pressure, just lightly.*

- *Do not be in a rush or set a time frame, remember the spirit world have to work at blending with you.*

In the beginning the writing may not be legible, this will improve with practise.

You can try with your eyes open or shut whatever feels most natural.

It is important not to allow your mind to interfere or attempt to make sense of what is expressed.

It is best to sit regularly at the same time, free from expectation or demands; by doing this you will enable the spirit communicator to achieve the most. When communication is authentic the information should be insightful, philosophical and at best highly evidential.

No matter what type of mediumistic expression you are experiencing it is vital to encourage an inner freedom. We are united by our hopes and aspirations as much as our doubts and collective unconscious fears. It is important to cultivate a strong attitude of mind where we can reach out to the spirit world and be the best we can. When fear closes a door love perceives a way, as very often our mind and our thinking can limit the potential of our mediumship from being fully realised.

HELPFUL POINTERS

- Always make the choice to begin a communication from a place of 'love rather than fear, belief rather than doubt'.

- Allow your mediumship natural expression, you are unique.

- Mediumship works at its best when there is no conscious effort to interfere with the communication.

- It is important to enter into the flow of communication as soon as you experience a sense of the presence of the spirit. If you wait too long it makes it harder for the spirit communicator to sustain the connection.

- There is no route map to the spirit, the communicators simply respond to the loving intent of the medium. The very nature of communication means the information will be variable, try not to compare. Just because you have experienced a different depth within the communication that doesn't mean it's not as good – it is just different.

- Never feel unworthy or not good enough, in the eyes of the spirit all are equal and one.

- Resist the mind's temptation to make sense of the information, otherwise you can alter what was essentially accurate information.

- Remember it is the spirit communicator's job to provide the information, don't search for information they are not prepared to give.

- Do not make a chore of your mediumship, the spirit want you to enjoy being their channel and to love liberating people from the fear of death.

- Your mediumship will change and develop as your understanding evolves.

- Stay true to what you have experienced, never alter what you have given to suit the person who receives the communication.

DEVELOPMENT CIRCLES AND THERE VALUE.

"In a circle, we are all equal,

There is no one in front of you

And there is nobody behind you

No one is above you or below you

Has neither beginning or ending

The circle is sacred because it it is designed to create unity".

Lakota Wisdom

In the past a development circle was considered the backbone of spiritualism and it is in the home circle where it really all began. It has enriched the lives of many who have attended, countless mediums have developed their innate potential and lifetime friendships have been forged.

A well-run circle is magical. Meeting together with other like-minded people, in the presence of spirit companions, is truly a treasure to behold and in every sense and meaning of the word is a journey of discovery.

Needless to say, a lot of indigenous cultures have used the circle to hold sacred meetings and to converse with spiritual realms; in meeting together visions would be encountered, prophecies foretold, and chants and prayers would be sent heavenward in the hope that these sacred utterances would be heard and invoke the blessings of whatever god was believed in, according to their respective religion. The power of a circle, I believe, is an intuitive knowledge inherent in man.

It Is important in any development circle that you run or join, that the right people participate. A sacred balance of giving and receiving should be the motive in the hearts of all who attend. To freely give to the advantage of another person's spiritual progression, means a natural enrichment of your own spiritual nature in the great circle of life, what we give is the measure of what we too shall receive. For life is ultimately not necessarily what we may feel has been accomplished, but how much we have lifted others up along the way.

The first consideration is towards making sure everyone attending has the capacity to put aside all the troubles of their everyday material life, it is not very helpful if a sitter's mind is fixed on all their anxieties as the energy each person brings as an offering of their presence is vital to the very best being achieved.

I was always taught that to begin with a sincere prayer enhances the energy and sets the tone. A circle should not be about taking people on a journey up a mountain or indeed over a rainbow into a fluffy cloud. A visualisation journey such as this unfortunately serves no purpose and is better left to a beginners' meditation group. As the sole aim is to create a power where the presence of the spirit may be felt and experienced by all present.

Some people prefer music, and it is true that music can help uplift the mind into other realms beyond the ordinary and daily routine, but I personally believe silence is the most conducive. If you are unsure, it might be an idea just to play a little preferred music for the first few moments to help clear the minds of those present and then sit in silence.

Discipline is important and helps to create a pattern of continuity. So, try as far as possible to ensure everyone is able to sit at the same day every

MEDIUMSHIP TOUCHING THE STARS

week and make a commitment. In the circle I sat in for many years when we used to set up an infra-red camera, on play back we found there was a lot of energetic activity leading up to the time before we actually sat, on reflection I felt this was possibly the activity and co-operation of spirit, preparing the atmosphere before we had even begun.

Ground rules should be made, such as relaying the importance when someone else is practising that they deserve everyone's attention. It is not appropriate to have someone trying to perceive a spirit presence, when it is not their turn and is not just unfair but dissipates the energy. There is no need to waste precious time visualising opening and closing chakras, which in the imagination conjures up a wild array of images. This energy system, though real, as the early Vedantic teaching states, is I believe beyond anyone's ability to control at will and scare-mongering stories, such as holes and tears in chakras, only create fear in people's minds. The chakras reflect the balance, flow and distribution of energy throughout our body and a well-balanced individual who has taken care to nourish, spirit, body and mind and be in touch with their emotional self, will have a harmonious flow of energy in these centres. This is I believe one situation where the saying 'a little knowledge is a dangerous thing' applies. The great mediums that make up our past demonstrated the art and grace of mediumistic communication in all its varying forms, before they had ever heard of the meaning of the word chakra and yet the power was beautifully and strongly expressed for all to witness.

Over the years I have met Swamis from the Hindu tradition, beautiful souls and some with remarkable powers, who in addition really had a wealth of understanding regarding these areas. One Swami in particular that I recall, had spent time in an Ashram with Mahatma Gandhi and had also sat for over twenty years in the Himalayas meditating in total seclusion. His rarefied lifestyle and years in meditation meant he could perceive these energy systems and how they functioned but for most of us, I believe, we still have a long way to go. Always question for yourself when you are told something is true, just because someone can tell you a few pieces of information regarding your life or even your state of health doesn't mean they know everything; in the end giving of information in this manner proves very little, but unfortunately human nature is such that people often instantly believe every word they are told, failing to question the reason how or why.

Once you have laid down your ground rules, it is essential at the beginning that everyone present should inwardly join together, in an atmosphere of harmony, and set the intent to focus on the same aim. Begin by connecting with the power of love. Encourage each person to identify, where within they experience love. If anyone finds this a little difficult, suggest they gently allow their attention to focus on whoever or whatever they associate love with. It may be a person, a member of their family or partner, God, the spirit world, or even a spiritual teacher, in fact, anything that evokes a deep sense of feeling within. Everyone has someone or something that will encourage a sense of love, it doesn't matter the nature of who or what, just the outcome, which is simply to be present in love.

When a feeling of loving energy has been created by all present, a noticeable change in the atmosphere in the room should be experienced. Now ask everyone to direct the love to the person sitting next to them on their right-hand side and send the energy round to each person in an anti-clockwise direction. Until it returns back full circle, creating an invisible energy uniting all. The reason behind this practice is to unite each person together as one whole. Notice how everybody coming together with the same aim really begins to have an empowering effect!

As the atmosphere begins to become charged with the power and presence of the spirit, a change in the temperature of the room is sometimes experi-enced often by becoming much colder, this was commonly called 'psychic breezes' years ago. The power that has been created makes it become easier for those developing to make a connection with the spirit world.

At this point the intention can be moved away from 'helping to build the power' to now 'actively using the power'. The person leading the circle, using their mediumistic power of awareness, should ask whoever they believe to be most receptive at this particular moment to make a contact with the spirit. It is important to be aware that the spirit communicators have to work using your mediumistic senses. Any thoughts, feelings or impressions experienced should be shared and then an effort to place the communication should follow.

Once this has been achieved the person leading the circle can move on to another member of the group and give the next person an opportunity to use their mediumistic powers to become aware of the presence of the spirit. Unless it is a trance development circle, most present should get an opportunity to practise at each session.

The power can be directed in any way you feel inwardly right. If you are wanting to run a circle to help encourage any trance potential, it is normal that just one person is focused on at any given time. Although bearing in mind the location of where you live and the occasional lack of availability of development circles, it may be necessary to divide the time equally between more than one person.

Sometimes those people who want to develop most aren't always the ones who actually develop first, so can I suggest that you listen to both the energy in the group and also the spirit world. Our will should become the will of the spirit and, if listened to and followed, each member will find their own development unfolding at a time that is right and fitting for them. It will soon become apparent who is at the stage in their development when conditions are right for their abilities to blossom.

Healing circles are very popular at the moment, which I think is both beautiful and very necessary. To meet together to deepen ability in order to be the channel for healing energy, by directing the power to an individual or for the greater good of the whole, will benefit everyone. These circles become power houses for the spirit world to be able to make a difference, for it has been said by the spirit in the trance states that they can only work in cooperation with those here on earth, it is not possible to intervene unless they have first been asked. We are the bridge between heaven and earth and the spirit world need us as much as we need them.

Sometimes it is not within the power of any spiritual healer or group to stop someone from passing, it is important at these times to realise there is indeed 'a time to be born and a time to die' as the saying goes. So please don't think you have failed if someone you have been directing your healing prayers towards passes. Possibly at the very least, by the grace of your efforts and love, you have improved the person's quality of life and helped them surrender to the process of letting go and enabled a gift in bringing about ease and dignity to the process dying. We can never judge the good that may have been achieved. It is not for any of us to change the course of human destiny.

It has become customary that a development circle should be run by a medium who has already worked for a considerable time and knows how to perceive when a student is really connecting with the presence of the spirit. In addition, the power that the medium has cultivated and worked with is utilised by the spirit to enable others to develop. The analogy of charging the flat battery of a car from one that is fully charged, to enable the car to have enough power to run on its own, is a good example.

It is believed in many spiritual traditions that just to be in the presence of someone who has awakened the power within has a very beneficial effect on those in their presence. This is why traditionally those seeking realisation, or liberation, and to inwardly move beyond the illusions of life commonly search for a spiritual teacher or Guru; inherent in man is the understanding of the beneficial effect of doing so. In the 1960s it was particularly common, and still is today, for people to go to India in search of a spiritual teacher. Even the Beatles found a new dimension to their lives from meeting Maharishi Mahesh Yogi, who introduced them to transcendental Meditation.

OSMOSIS

The spiritual teacher, Ramana, has influenced countless people on their spiritual journey. Ramana's practice was recognised to be what is called a process of osmosis. For he would remain in the silence and the flow of his spiritual power would be transmitted to those in his presence; this power transference was recognised to be of the most direct and concentrated form, creating a significant change within the awareness of those present, resulting in a profound spiritual transformation.

Intriguingly, a medium called Catherine Berry (1813-1891) who didn't actually develop her mediumship until later in her life when she was fifty years old, was known by other mediums for her extraordinary ability to transfer power in a similar way. It was a common practice that other mediums would ask to sit in her presence before they would demonstrate at a seance. She was considered to be able, through the transmission of power, to aid the development of other mediums. This conclusion was reached only after years of study of Catherine's work and the people she had helped.

Catherine's mediumistic abilities ranged from automatic writing and healing to include drawing and painting; in 1874 an exhibition of over five hundred of her watercolour paintings was held in Brighton, Sussex.

For many years I had wondered who the first medium was to come up with the idea of using a cabinet when sitting for physical mediumship; my curiosity was satisfied on researching the mediumship of Catherine Berry, when I found it stated that she was the first medium to receive the impression to sit for the spirit in this way, believing it would help contain the power and create a feeling of security for the medium.

EXERCISE

• When developing mediumship, it is helpful to encourage a greater connection with the language of feeling, as a large part of the communication is experienced in this way. Of course, no two mediums are ever the same, but it does help significantly to be in touch with the emotional side of your nature. If you are someone who tends to be very visual and find it hard to move into connecting with feeling, music can be a powerful tool. To contemplate music which evokes within you an emotional response can help you to become more receptive to your feelings.

• Listen to music with varying different themes and allow your awareness to be present within the feelings the music awakens. For within its power is the capacity to evoke memories buried within the soul, stir emotions, transport us to a different time and place long forgotten and stir the heart to feel in our deepest essence. Over the centuries, music has been the source of inspiration and can free and liberate unexpressed emotion, enabling it to move through us to nourish the soul as a river of energy.

• Next find someone who is willing for you to practise with them. Offer the intent to the spirit to bring forward a song which will have emotional significance and evoke a particular memory for the spirit and the sitter. Explore this in as much detail as possible, allowing yourself to not judge the information but inwardly move with the flow of the communication, being open and receptive to the story the spirit communicator is sharing about themselves and the journey of their life. This can range from childhood days, meaningful events in a relationship, weddings and anniversaries, there is no limit as to the content which has the potential to be conveyed in this way; you may even find the spirit person may give you more than one song, if they are creative, a song may be given

168

for different stages in their life or even different emotions.

* Contemplate: When listening to music, ask yourself if the emotion of sadness or joy is in the music or in you?

Reference:

Encyclopedia of Psychic Science by Nandor Fodor, Arthurs Press 1933

Medium of the Century by Chico Xavier, Round Table Publishing

Further reading:

Is There an Afterlife? By David Fontana, O-Books.net

MEDIUMSHIP TOUCHING THE STARS

CHAPTER EIGHT

PROPHECY

AND ITS RELEVANCE TO MEDIUMSHIP

"The gift of vision belongs to all. It links man to the world he lives in and by virtue of its magic not only permits him to uncover the secrets of nature herself, but may someday enable him to wrest the deep meaning of creation from the universe".

Eileen Garrett

Prophecy is truly a natural expression of mediumistic powers. Yet although not encouraged today, is part of the rich and diverse heritage in the lineage of spiritualism. Understandably prophecy is not considered to be proof of survival until the prophecy is fulfilled and of course then it becomes the truth and a reflection of the power and presence of the spirit.

Every holy book that has ever been written, including the bible, is filled with the visions and prophecies from those who at the time fulfilled the role of oracle or prophet, their wise council was frequently sought, and their visions often manifested as true with the passing of time. These historic prophesies came from as diverse sources as the Greek oracles, the prophets in Egyptian temples, the visionary shamans of indigenous tribes and the Celtic mystics who were called seers. Even Buddhism's highest regions of Tibet echoed, with divine accuracy, the prediction of the birthplace of the next Dalai Lama. Through the spoken word to the wonder of images and visions being played out like some sacred film, prophesy is a mystery that has intrigued mankind.

If you have ever been asked by someone you meet for the first time, "What do you do?" and replied, "I work as a medium", then you are a brave person. You can guarantee a reply, in fact I can hear it now, as I have been asked it so many times, "Then can you tell me the lottery numbers". It just doesn't work in that way and if it did wouldn't we all be first in the queue, the line forms to the right! The implications of winning may change the destiny of those whom you have chosen to share it with and could have vast implications in redirecting the course of not only your own life, but others as well. If you think about it for a moment the consequences are enormous, it's like playing with the universe.

Have you ever been told something from a spiritual medium which despite any unlikely possibility at the time later came true? It's quite mind-blowing that this is possible but can really make someone take a leap in their thinking! Fundamentally more important is how do the spirit communicators know this, in the first place, and does it then mean all that we can consider to be unknown is really known!

I personally believe prophecy has a role to play, after all, mediums have frequently been accused of merely mind reading. I have found that two aspects of communication can distinctly disprove this concept; the first one

172

being when a medium gives information not known by the sitter, which they need to go and ask another member of the family to validate and the second is prophecy, which totally disproves the mind reading theory. I have come to realise that sometimes relaying information a person already knows to be true doesn't have quite the same impact as imparting information that has not yet come to pass. When this does happen, it facilitates taking the person on a journey to new shores and horizons of possibility and awakening.

Mediums are not, of course, fortune tellers. Although frequently within the power and presence of the spirit, those in the great beyond have an uncanny way of giving insightful and accurate information of events that have not yet happened, but only if the intelligence of those in spirit feel it appropriate, born from a desire to bring reassurance or to give hope that present circumstances will pass. However, those in spirit cannot, on demand, comply with our requests. It must be the will of the spirit, and not our will, that pre-empts the possibility of insight, enabling what is natural and right to be revealed.

As I have previously suggested, as the spirit are not bound by time they are not restricted by time. As the medium Eileen Garrett once said, "In the clairvoyant reality, there is no past, no present and no future, all is one vast whole and within that whole it is the relationship that one thing has to another that is deemed most relevant". I rather like Eileen's explanation and to me it makes sense that we must always apply a discerning attitude to information we are given and question for ourselves. Yet it is only here at this material level on earth that our life has to be defined by the flow of time, of past, present and future; as a spiritual being we are non-local and timeless. So, it is possible that, to our spiritual self, everything is experienced outside of time, making prophecy possible.

Many mediums have been known for their gift of prophecy, including Bertha Harris, Eileen Garrett, Albert Best, Gordon Higginson, William Stead, Edgar

173

Cayce and countless others. Even the artist Leonardo Da Vinci made remarkable prophecies, describing future inventions and discoveries that came to pass. It's as though spiritual vision reveals a glimpse into other possibilities of futures not yet born and yet the seed of potentiality already exists.

The remarkable prophecy, given by the exceptional medium Annie Brittain comes to mind. For during a demonstration, she gave a communication to a very young Fanny Higginson from her Mother, who she had left at home, alive and well before she attended the service. Declaring that whilst she had been there at the church her mother had passed and foretold that she would one day be a medium. She stated she would have a son who would follow in her footsteps and the name of Higginson would be associated with Spiritualism for over one hundred years.

The prediction of course came true, as no sooner had she arrived home but was met by the news her mother had indeed passed and true to the prophecy, went on to become a medium herself. Gordon's mediumistic powers shaped the history of spiritualism as he became the finest exponent of mediumship the world has ever known.

The extraordinary medium Vincent Turvey, in his book The Beginnings of Seership, published over one hundred years ago when spiritualism was still in its earlier days, describes his ability to project his consciousness to another place through what he termed 'mental body travelling and prophecy', considered his abilities to be 'God consciousness', or the realisation or attainment of the self.

Vincent Turvey was frequently known to answer letters from people inquiring after passed loved ones, as though you would inquire of someone still living, which they are of course! It was a common occurrence as part of the

174

request that he would be asked to foretell an outcome to events which may have been troubling the person greatly. This he willingly made an attempt to do, if it was to eliminate the burden of anxiety. Another remarkable ability he had was that, when speaking to a person by phone, he could easily and with great precision give an account of the person's home and sometimes even visitors that were present at the time. This he called 'phone-voyance'.

Such are the extraordinary abilities in every shape and form of those who have gone before us, who moved through the boundaries of the conditioned self into new realms of possibility.

The prophetic experience often awakens an ability to see, hear and feel deep emotion directly connected to the vision. This is a process of 'knowing through being', sometimes momentarily as though you were living it yourself, others as though a glimpse of a future time is unravelling before your awareness. It is as though we have become a spectator, an observer and the experience is flowing to us.

When a person isn't actively using their mediumistic powers of awareness it is common for the spirit to communicate in and through the language of dreams. It is a way of utilising the opportunity to access the attention of the person through the unconscious mind. On waking there is sometimes a recollection of the message conveyed, particularly when the information has occurred during the phase of sleep when our consciousness is starting to identify with the perception of worldly sensory awareness once more.

In the past I have had many dreams of communicating with spirit friends and loved ones, sometimes with such clarity that specific details were given, it was as though the spirit wanted to reassure me of their continued existence by relaying information of future events. It leaves the person who has experienced this type of communication with an unmistakable feeling of the authenticity of what has taken place, but of course only the passing of time will invariably prove whether the future details occur.

The inventor Thomas Edison once said, "Never go to sleep without a request to your subconscious mind". This suggestion can be used to obtain assistance with finding a resolution to a problem, to provide some creative ideas on what direction to take in life or, alternatively, to receive insight from those in the spirit. Why don't you give it a try?

Before you go to sleep, offer your intent to those you know in the spirit world that you may be aware of them and, on waking, you might find that you will have a recollection of the experience. You could even experiment by asking for specific proof of their reality by foretelling a future outcome or event in your life. Normally the spirit are happy to experiment in such a way, if it helps to prove their continued presence.

If prophecy is possible does it then mean that our lives are already mapped out for each of us and this predisposes the question, "Is there such a thing as freedom of choice or free will?". I am of the opinion that when we are born, we have a blueprint or a map of life events, particular situations the soul has agreed to experience and people to meet, all necessary for our greater growth, and particular lessons that we need to learn. This is similar to signing up for a specific course of study. Ultimately, we need to experience whatever it is we agreed to learn, the choice is do we take the road to the right, or to the left, yet each route ends up at the same destination. A little like going on a journey in a car, do you choose the motorway, which is potentially faster, but may end up with hold-ups and tailbacks, or the slower, but more scenic, country road with the possibility of getting stuck behind a tractor; the possibility is that each may have its own delays and positive experiences, but ultimately you arrive at your journey's end come what may.

EXERCISE

For experimenting and teaching purposes

- Begin by asking a friend to write down a question concerning their future, or the particular outcome of events in their life. Then get them to place the question in an envelope. It's important that you do not to know what the question is.

- Make an offering to the spirit world that they may help you to explore prophecy, bearing in mind we can never demand of the spirit.

- Sit quietly and allow the mind to become focused, bring all of your awareness to a central point of gaze.

- Hold your attention here as long as you can without becoming mentally tired, while still feeling relaxed. Feel a sense of love in your heart.

- Set the intent and invite the possibility that the spirit communicator may be able to relay the answer to the question, either through the language of feeling, hearing, seeing, sensing, or knowing.

- Of course, it is important to validate the spirit person's reality first, so you will need to establish who is communicating by providing as much information as possible; personality, appearance, nature of passing, shared memories, really allowing yourself to become immersed in the presence of the spirit.

- Become receptive to the flow of feelings and impressions that touch your awareness.

- Try to be detached - this is essential so that you can easily discern the difference between your imagination and actually receiving.

- Share all you have experienced, but additionally write down any feelings or images you may have received, as this is important for future reference.

- If you have relayed a spirit communicator with accuracy, their presence has been identified and any information given understood then you can feel confident in trusting any further information they may care to give. Now all you need to do is wait!

- It is normally true that whenever we try to explore possibilities or experiment in order to learn, the spirit world seem to enjoy the opportunity, if it ultimately helps in proving the reality of their continued existence.

- Alternatively, try projecting your consciousness to the home of someone you know but have never visited.

- Inform the person of your intention, of course, and arrange a time that you can both connect. Make sure you don't rush but pay attention to detail, with your spiritual powers of awareness. Visualise yourself at the door of your friend's home, describe the door, what type of texture notice any feelings which may arise. Observe the surroundings. Pay attention to as much detail as possible. What colours do you sense or see? Once you have explored this as much as possible, contact your friend and compare what you have experienced to see how much is actually true!

- Some people call this mind travelling and there have, in the past, been lots of experiments done in this area. Try to mind travel to a place that you have never been to before, just make sure that afterwards you can research the details regarding the interior of the building or topography of the landscape, so that it can be easily validated.

- These different methods help prove that your conscious awareness is not restricted to the physicality of the body and that consciousness doesn't necessarily function in time.

- If you should ever receive information through a medium from a spirit loved one about something that hasn't happened yet, it's a good idea to take note of the date and the content of the information and go over it from time to time, to find out just how much information actually came true.

THE FOUR QUARTETS

Burnt Norton

Time past and time future

Allow but a little consciousness

To be conscious is not to be in time

But only in time can the moment in the rose garden

The moment in the arbour where the rain beat

The moment in the drafty church at smoke fall

Be remembered; involved with past and future

Only through time is time conquered.

T.S Elliot

Reference:

Awareness by Eileen Garrett, Parapsychology Foundation

CHAPTER NINE

THE TRANCE STATES EXPLAINED

I saw eternity the other night,

Like a great ring of pure and endless light,

All calm as it was bright.

'Henry Vaughan'

The trance states are a natural progression of mediumistic awareness and occur when the spirit and medium come together as one, as a blending. Just as a flower blooms when conditions are right, the same applies to all mediumship, if the medium learns the art of merely becoming the channel and of surrendering to those in the spirit. This passive condition of simply allowing, creates a receptivity within the medium whereby timeless wisdom and philosophy of the spirit can be expressed. Philosophy which can be the source of insight, help facilitate inner growth and, if applied to the day to day living of life, can be tools to assist each on our spiritual journey.

Any time a medium works in co-operation with the spirit world it is true to say the medium is experiencing a state of entrancement, within which there are many stages and levels. The spirit influences blend through the auric energies and never enter the physical body, as has been described by some in the past. It is always dignified - a graceful passage of blending one with the other. Yet it additionally requires the medium to have both a rational and disciplined mind. These heightened states are not a single point of destination or arrival, but instead a moving of the mind towards an expansion, whereby we move inwardly from our limited everyday conscious-ness, to experience a state of awareness and universal consciousness is achieved. The result of this process is to be at one with the spirit and the totality of life itself.

Patience and the removal of expectation of a desired result will enhance any natural abilities as they become apparent, the unfoldment of the trance states cannot be rushed. Allowing yourself time just to enjoy the experience of blending and to realise when you sit in the presence of the spirit you bring something back with you which, even though invisible, is nonetheless real. Enrichment of soul and a transference of power is encountered when we create an inner space to meet the spirit world, in love and oneness of being.

THE THREE FORMS OF DISTRACTION WHEN SITTING FOR THE TRANCE STATES

The first form of distraction is the body.

Sometimes there are unfamiliar feelings which may arise, apart from the heart rate momentarily becoming more rapid as a deepening blending takes place, other unusual sensations can be experienced. A physical feeling of nausea can occur in the stomach or solar plexus when energy is being drawn. Take this to be a positive sign that something is really happening.

The second is your perception.

As your awareness begins to heighten it is common to feel as though you are expanding one moment and shrinking the next. I have often had the feeling that the chair I am sitting on has become fluid this I believe to be caused by perception being experienced through your spiritual powers of awareness rather than your physical senses. Sometimes it is as though your spatial awareness has altered and your consciousness is no longer confined to, or located in, your body. Of course, your consciousness is in reality not bound to the limitations of your physical self, it only appears that way.

The third distraction is the mind.

Needless to say, the mind creates its own resistance to the trance states for, apart from having by its very nature an intrinsic desire to make sense of and translate every feeling and experience, has a natural tendency to want to be in control. To learn the subtle yet necessary ability of relinquishing control is extremely important to assist the freeing of the mind in order to surrender to the spirit influence.

Learning the art of becoming passive and quietening the rational mind is important as a gradual process of blending takes place, frequently reflected by a subtle change in the natural rhythm of the breath. It is as though the medium is inwardly realigning with universal consciousness, with the power of unseen worlds, and this may manifest through the breath. Nothing exaggerated, but a gentle altering is often experienced. This process happens slowly as the medium needs to learn the art of surrender and the grace of letting go. Any effort to remain in control by the mind of the medium will impede the efforts of the spirit. The blending must be just right otherwise the moment will pass, and the opportunity lost until the next time.

If you have ever watched someone practising the art of Tai Chi you will witness the grace of 'allowing' in action. Each movement flows gently into the next, this is a perfect example of allowing, and not creating resistance. To try means to apply effort and when there is significant effort there will also be tension. The energy created by tension is rigid and is not conducive to facilitating the altered states, for to surrender means taking the path of least resistance and this can only happen when there is both relaxation of the body and freedom of the mind.

The trance states however are not simply speaking with your eyes closed, sometimes people have a tendency to think this is all that is necessary. Although trance may on the surface appear to be only too easy, there is a degree of natural ability and a great deal of patience required. If you ever encounter a medium giving a demonstration of trance and within a few seconds start speaking, it is more than likely that the speech is arising from the mind of the medium and not the spirit. Trance states are always gradual and rarely, if ever, instant. One exception to the rule is the Seth teachings through the medium Jane Roberts. Interestingly, Jane didn't even believe in life after death and took some convincing as to the reality of what was taking place and initially thought that it was the manifestation of her subconscious mind, as I am sure anyone not having an understanding of the nature of communication would naturally do. Yet when you look at the content of her trance sessions and the level of knowledge expressed it is apparent this is beyond the understanding of the medium in waking consciousness. Additionally, the authenticity of Jane's abilities was supported by the entire presence mannerisms, demeanour, pronunciation of words, which remained consistent throughout long sessions, and knowledge of varying topics. This, I may add, is rare and certainly would be classed as not the norm within most schools of mediumistic development.

Revealing indications that there is too much involvement of the mind of the medium can often be seen when there is continual reference to the medium in a personal manner. Another is the need to ask those present if they have a question immediately, as why would those in the spirit make all the effort just to pop in and say, "Have you got a question?" At this stage it is important to observe if there is any substance or depth regarding what is being said. The intelligence of the spirit world is such that questions of those present are often answered within the philosophy expressed; it's as though they can perceive our innermost thoughts before a word has even been uttered. Additionally, exaggerated movement of the medium is also a reflection of the lack of authenticity, movement of the body will only locate awareness and attention within the physical self and is not conducive to freeing the mind.

Be aware of the quality of your thoughts, as our thoughts are the architects of our reality and shape or mould each new experience; this is as much true in the inner life as the outer. We meet in the universe not only what we expect but also what we create for ourselves. Total belief and trust in the spirit realities and your own self will serve you well and transfer you inwardly from the realms of belief to pure knowing. Frequently people say they believe in the spirit world but fail to believe in their own self, we are spirit here and now and belong to this other realm of being. To deny one means to simply deny the other!

Trust is paramount and invariably people have a problem regarding trusting their own selves. It requires less mental effort to doubt rather than believe, but trust is its own reward and significantly enhances the blending. As a baby making our entrance into the world and leaving the security of our mother, our first experience is to trust in the unknown and that our physical life will not fail us. Our mediumistic nature requires each of us to move into the unknown, but realising as we do so that the spirit will not disappoint us, just as in being born to this world provides all that is required for nourishment of the soul, the relationship with those in the unseen world was forged long before we chose to be born.

Just as loving requires us to be vulnerable, the altered states are the same. Up to this point, everything we have done in our lives has necessitated the need to be in charge, so relinquishing control is not easy for most of us. If the voice of the spirit is to be expressed through you, it will require the greatest yet simplest challenge, that you learn the art of surrender. Easier said than done, you may be thinking!

Everything expressed in the trance states should always enrich and inspire in some way. Anything of the opposite nature is normally coming from the subconscious mind of the medium. Throughout the many years of communication between those on the spirit side of life and here, unspoken ethics exist; appropriate conduct which flows from age to age. The articulation of thought flow from spirit will always leave the recipient with a feeling of enhanced wellbeing and peace. It's as though you have witnessed something sacred and been in the presence of pure love. As the respected trance medium J. J. Morse stated, "The trance state is the doorway to the spirit world, where the higher capacities of human nature reside. The trance state is the key used to transcend the environment of mortality and ascend into the domain of spirituality".

Never will those in the world unseen judge us, demand or dictate how we should be living our life. It is not for them to make all our decisions for us. Why should it be upon their shoulders to bear the responsibility of what is rightfully ours. To do so, by its very nature would take away freedom of choice. There exist in the universe natural spiritual laws to which all, irrespective of level or dimension of life, are bound.

On the same note, when a communication is authentic there is never a need from the spirit perspective to announce who they are. Fancy titles and famous names are rarely from the spirit; on the contrary, these are frequently a by-product of the ego, arising from the needs of the medium on a sub-conscious level rather than the spirit. "By their fruits we shall know them", Matthew 7:16, is as true today as when it first appeared in the Bible. For it soon becomes evident when you are bearing witness to the presence of the spirit, that the quality of what is expressed and the way it is delivered becomes a testament to the truth, for each word spoken will resonate deep within and touch your soul. Feeling is its own language. In other words, you know it when you experience a genuine communion between heaven and earth.

Over-helpful sitters, although well meaning, should be discouraged from direct requests It is extremely important not to ask questions such as "who are you and what is your name' as soon as the spirit begins to get comfortable using their medium. This sort of specific questioning should be avoided, as to bombard the spirit with a hundred questions will only serve to bring the awareness of the medium rushing back.

The benefits of the trance states are enormous, not only will they leave a residual power within the medium but also enhance all other latent faculties of the sensitive. It becomes apparent that all the wisdom expressed in the trance states becomes an integral part of waking consciousness and an enrichment of soul occurs.

It is normal by measure of varying degrees to hear what is being said in the initial stages of unfoldment. Once the spirit influences have learnt to master the art of blending with the medium a sense of trust and reassurance is created and confidence in the entire process can be achieved, this facilitates a deepening of the medium's ability to freely move with the experience, without reservation.

The longer the trance state is maintained by the spirit influences, the greater the possibility of the medium feeling completely removed from the experience. It can be as though you are the observer listening in or witnessing the proceedings from above or behind your physical self. Frequently a feeling of spaciousness is experienced, of no longer being located to the confines of your physical self, until only fragments of what has been said are heard, as if the experience is all happening in the distance and the medium is not a part of it.

There is very little deep trance mediumship today. With the exception of a few and of course those rare souls who work within the realms of physical mediumship. I believe the spirit world have been perfecting working through their sensitives, mastering the art of enabling their thought flow to be expressed without the need to take the medium to an unconscious state, where a loud noise or disturbance could potentially create a shock to the nervous system and the medium being left with an uncomfortable feeling of being displaced.

Mediumship at its best takes place when the medium has simply mastered the art of getting their own self out of the way, enabling the undiluted message of the spirit to be expressed.

How can the medium know for sure when the trance state is genuine and what is conveyed has its origin in the intelligent presence of those in other realms? This is a question which frequently arises from the enquiring and discriminating mind of both the medium and observer. If pondered on for too long this can create its own obstacle. As all relationships should be founded on trust, this is even more imperative with our dealing with those in the spirit world. To continually question "is it me or the spirit?" is the age-old dilemma which all mediums at various stages of their spiritual journey have asked. Even the exceptional trance medium Eileen Garrett, after a lifetime of research and study into the nature of her own mediumship, expressed uncertainty even though the most remarkable proof had been relayed on many occasions. I have thought about this often and think that possibly it is due to the fact that those who influence from the spirit side of life become, over the years, such a part of us that a deep familiarity develops and so the separation becomes less distinct. After all, we live in a vast ocean of consciousness. We fail to see the place where the river merges with the sea, as one blends with the other.

Unfortunately, we live in a society where people are becoming conditioned into expecting instant results so many give up, I am sure, when success is just around the corner because we cannot measure results in these areas of experience or truly comprehend the enormous effort those in the unseen world make on our behalf. A genuine seeker will be happy to sit without the baggage of expectations or a list of demands. Just to sit for the joy of sitting in the presence of those in the spirit world and to be immersed in the presence of love is truly its own reward.

Just as a cup fills drop by drop until one last drop makes it overflow, it is true to say it wasn't just the last drop, but each drop that had gone before, one day when you least expect it your cup will overflow and all that you had been working towards manifests, so don't stop just because you have not experienced any obvious results, as you can never tell when the moment may occur that enables progression.

Differences occur within the blending and vary from one person to another and the mind, by its very nature, will always seek comparison. Sometimes in the delivery of a trance talk, the voice may vary slightly, or even greatly, from that of the medium in normal waking consciousness. But often the voice may not vary at all. No one way is right or wrong or, even, better. Learning to accept that whatever happens is the way that is right for you is helpful. When the power is strong the spirit control often influences the voice box so a moderate change can be heard, but it all depends on the natural ability of the medium.

If you have cultivated trust, then it will be much easier for you, as a medium, to surrender to the stream of thoughts that can move through your mind before the spirit influences master control. A gentle co-operation will benefit both the medium and the spirit, as the effort from the spirit needs to be met with the least resistance. This is because sometimes when we don't even realise, and with the best will in the world, subconscious fears or doubts can and do create an energetic wall or barrier. If no progress is being made it is helpful to ask yourself honestly if there are any doubts or fears that may be preventing you from being the channel for the spirit.

The connection may begin with one word or a sentence, or in some cases no awareness whatsoever of any feelings or thoughts. The moment something is voiced the journey can begin and a relationship is forged. No one way is right or wrong. It is just different and will vary accordingly to the nature of the mind and abilities of the medium involved. No two people are the same and what works for one may differ with another. How we each respond to the influence of the spirit will vary according to our own individual sensitivity and receptivity.

TRANCE COMMUNICATION

This particular type of mediumship is rare and can best be described as loved ones speaking directly through the medium. There are fewer people now who have this level of ability and can be likened to sitting in a room in the presence of a loved one again, having a direct conversation with them. It is, I believe, a big thing to ask of our spirit relatives, as I am sure they have to master the art of communicating in a deeper way, as much as those on this side of life do, in addition to having to go through the ordeal of being so close to this level once more and mastering the art of blending with the medium.

PHILOSOPHY OF THE SPIRIT

To learn the art of withdrawing your awareness from the external world and any mental activity, aspiring to still both body and mind will enhance any latent abilities. Usually, the trance states are a form of conveying the philosophy from those in the spirit world and a talk is given which should be intelligent, articulate and enriching. The delivery, infliction and phraseology would normally differ from those of the medium and thus the presence of the spirit should be experienced by those present. No-one can manufacture the feeling which makes the atmosphere become charged, as though it is imbued with what can only be likened to an electrical power and a feeling of almost overwhelming love.

ART IN THE TRANCE STATES

This is an incredible ability where the medium, through an altered state, is influenced by the spirit to such a deep level that the spirit can paint through the medium. Scottish born David Duguid's mediumistic abilities were extraordinary, as through him miniature oil paintings were produced by the spirit in complete darkness. May and Lizzie Bangs, known as the 'Bangs sisters', would go into an altered state with the spirit drawing upon the power the two sisters provided. The spirit would then paint remarkable portraits onto a canvas without it being physically touched, of spirit loved ones for those present. This is known as precipitated spirit art; it is said that the invisible hands painted the portraits with remarkable likeness to the actual loved

191

ones. The portraits would invariably begin with eyes being painted on the canvas first, on being analysed the painting medium used was of no known earthly substance but very closely resembled the dust on butterfly wings.

It is common that art done in this manner is normally of a very fast speed in comparison with someone working in a normal state of conscious awareness.

TRANCE HEALING

Real trance healers are rare now and differ from normal spiritual healers, in as much as the healing medium is immersed totally in the presence of a spirit influence whose sole purpose is to blend with the medium to a greater depth, enabling healing to be transferred in a more powerful way. In the past, healing through the presence of the spirit world be performed in what would commonly be called miracles. Trance healers who worked in this way included William Henry Lilley, Isa Northage and George Chapman.

EXPLORING TRANCE STATES

• *Make sure you are sitting in a place where you won't be disturbed.*

• *Allow your awareness to focus on the breath, simply observing this involuntary response.*

• *Lovingly offer the intent to be used as a channel.*

• *Observe how without effort on your part the breath naturally slows and deepens.*

• *If at any time you become distracted don't worry, just realign your attention once more with the breath. Very often the heart rate temporarily quickens, this is proceeded by a natural slowing of the heart, followed by a significant deepening of the breath.*

- *The chattering of the mind stills as thoughts find a natural place of rest. The mind quietens, the breath deepens, the heart slows.*

- *When a passive state both within and without has been achieved, spirit with spirit can meet.*

- *The more you surrender and allow yourself to inwardly move aside, the greater will be the influence of the spirit.*

- *The information passes through you, rather than from you, and invariably the depth of communication should exceed the knowledge of the medium. Is the communication consistent, in both the quality and delivery? Is there an atmospheric change?*

- *As the trance states require the mind of the medium to be at rest, it is not necessary for the sensitive to be experiencing visual imagery; if this is happens, it generally means that the medium has become too involved and this is often propelled by a need to be seen to be doing something.*

- *In a situation where you are invited to give energy and power to support another and the spirit influence maintains a good degree of hold over the mind of the medium and begins to speak, it is best not to ask questions. All this will do is encourage the medium to bring their mind back into the experience and the same degree of blending will no longer be maintained.*

In my experience, the witnessing of the breath and observation of your own natural rhythm, although simple, is nevertheless helpful. Within the trance states if you use a complicated technique it often has the reverse effect by keeping the mind involved, your awareness to present. A balance of disarming the rational mind by the giving of a subtle task such as the observation of the process of breathing, will occupy the mind without the impact of making it too alert. Repetition and rhythm are always conducive. Which is why indigenous people performing spiritual ceremonies have in the past used chanting, drumming, gongs and movement to induce trance.

Whilst acknowledging that each culture has historically adopted its own most appropriate way of inducing a change in conscious states, we now realise that what is most important is a natural inward movement into grace and a gentle unfolding of each person's own innate abilities. In my experience love is the key; if we fix our heart and intent on love, the invisible becomes visible by the beauty of what is said and by the joy and comfort that is felt.

In fact, everything to do with our mediumistic nature should be simple - there is no need for complicated techniques or methods. Those 'old school' mediums, in the days when mediumship was at its finest, knew nothing other than to train themselves to be passive and listen to the spirit. By allowing themselves to be immersed in the power, to move with it, to feel, to perceive by being at one with the spirit, there was no room to doubt. People hear but they don't always listen, they look but don't always see, to be entirely present in the experience of really listening is vital to the cultivation of mediumistic powers of awareness.

EXERCISE

• If you are fortunate enough to have someone to sit for you to support your development, you might like to explore what is helpful in overcoming the mind's need to try to control what is taking place.

• The sitter should create a liminal space for the medium. Liminal originates from the Latin root 'limen' and signifies a threshold which simply represents a space where you have left something behind but have not arrived or experienced the new; it is a transition space. It exists as an invitation to surrender to all that was and embrace the new, trusting that you will be held and supported.

- To feel safe when sitting for the trance states is so important and enables the medium to feel free within the process whilst not being judged or pressured. Please put any expectations aside and don't visit them in your thoughts again.

- You, the medium, should start by allowing attention to be focused on a fixed point of gaze bringing all of your awareness and attention to this one place of seeing. Keeping your eyes open until, after intense concentration, the eyelids naturally become tired and want to close. This induces a gentle way of quietening the noisy chatter of the mind and you will find it enhances the ability to move into blending with the spirit with greater ease.

- The sitter offers to the spirit that they may receive a colour which will support the medium within the experience, that can mentally be sent to the medium. This assists in holding the attention on the medium and not allowing the mind to wonder, as so often, even with the best will and intent, people become distracted. An exchange of energy occurs between both the medium, the sitter and the spirit. A flow of energy moving in harmony from one to the other.

- Now a sacred space has been created, all the medium needs to do is inwardly invite a deeper blending with the spirit. Those who constantly help from the world unseen and are indeed our friends, offer within this moment the opportunity that they may help facilitate a surrendering, so they may find a voice through the medium in order that the purest teachings may be expressed.

- The power always finds its own level and normally becomes apparent when you have sat for long enough. At the end, even though nothing may have been said by the spirit, share all that has been experienced, as frequently a pattern emerges and becomes a way of giving reassurance to all concerned. The more familiar experiences occur, the easier it is to trust what is taking place. Energy, although it can't be seen, is nonetheless real; after all, belief is invisible and yet the impact of belief can blossom into awakening potential.

Further Reading:

Surgeon from another world by George Chapman and Roy Stemman

Silver Birch Speaks by Silvia Barbanell

Trance Mediumship by J.J. Morse, SDU publications

Wisdom of Ramadan by Ursula Roberts, Regency Press

Fifty Years a Medium by Estelle Roberts, SDU publications

Seth speaks by Jane Roberts, New World Library

CHAPTER TEN

GATHERED WISDOM

EXTRACTS FROM TRANCE TEACHINGS

In the universe there are things that are known

and things that are unknown and in

between there are doors.

William Blake, poet and mystic.

Over the years I have grown to love those dear souls who work through me; separate individuals who bring colour to my life and breathe the living word of the spirit into everything. Of course, each would say they have moved beyond the confines of nationality or a belief in any one chosen religion they may have once shared and now perceive existence from a broader perspective and that it would be appropriate to describe themselves as simply pure spirit. When communicating, however, they use a familiar form of expression, one which they are comfortable with. This, I am told by the spirit, helps to create in the mind of the listener an interest in what is being expressed and variety to hold their attention, enabling the timeless wisdom from the spirit world to be voiced once more and the sleeping memory of man's true nature rekindled into awakening.

Significant differences are apparent within the delivery and phraseology of the spirit teachings and this is due to the essence and colour of each influence communicating.

Surely the purpose of true spiritual mediumship is to lead mankind to the very threshold of the truth of our divine nature and the realisation that we are eternal beings. No longer do we need an intermediary between God and our own self, we are each God viewing existence from our respective reality. We are each a unique expression of divine power. The key is in each person's hands; we just need to open the door.

All the teachings below are collected over the long years that my spirit team have been using me as a channel. I am indebted to each one, as their presence has expanded the horizon of my understanding of life itself.

A CREED TO LIVE BY

Each person is a visitor upon the earth. Travellers passing by, nothing belongs to you. Even your physical body is borrowed from the universe and is comprised of stardust, particles of energy and elements of the earth. Your physical form is amassed from the genetic components of the vast lineage of your ancestors, but you do not own it. For one day when your earthly days are done it shall return, from whence it came.

Learn to respect and honour your physical body for it is the means by which your soul may express itself and come to know it's true nature, through the rich diversity of experience. Learn also to respect the earth for it is the garden of creation. Walk softly so your footsteps may kiss the earth with gentleness. Realise that everywhere is sacred and holy ground. Respectfully nurture all manner of life, for all creation exists for a reason, even when it is beyond your comprehension. Guard wisely the blessings of nature, for the trees and fruits of the forest should serve generations not yet born. For it is granted that each be custodians of today, so others may live abundantly tomorrow.

Learn to take in proportion to your needs and discern the difference between a need and greed. As you take, realise by the very act of taking, you also have an obligation to give, so ensuring the balance of creation may be sustained, whether materially or spiritually.

In the great circle of existence, the life of one is bound by unseen threads to the greater whole. To each is given a part to play, a reason to be born. Judge no one as better or lesser than yourself, for all are equal and born of the same breath of life, of the same fraternity of love. Walk in harmony with all, even though their thoughts may differ from your own and their skin be of a different tone.

For you are only a visitor upon the earth, just passing by. Ensure the world is the richer by measure of all you have freely given by the grace of your presence. So, as the great sun sets on the last day of your earthly life and the heavenly spaces call your spirit home, all of creation will sound your name with praise.

AWARENESS

Listen to the space between each breath

Listen to the space between each word

Until you can hear, what has not been said

And perceive with true awareness

The need in the heart of another

ACKNOWLEDGE.

Even the light of a thousand stars cannot compare to the infinite light of your own inner being. The flight of a thousand birds cannot compare to the freedom which is your own divine heritage. Why drink from one cup when the waters of the universe are yours. Why make yourself prisoners and throw away the key, you have fashioned the bars by your own making, from your self-created limitations when all the while you are free.

Learn to acknowledge your birth right, the power that created the stars in all their glory and the flowing rivers has crowned your consciousness with the vision to behold wonder and your heart to know love, so the song of the universe may flow through your veins and the miracle of creation know the splendour of your praise.

ALTAR

No man-made temple of stone or clay can ever compare to the temple of your own inner being. Therein enter every day and at the altar of the heart let yourself be cleansed of all that perplexes the spirit and troubles the soul. Close the door to the distractions of the outer world and allow the illumination of the divine to speak in the voiceless language of love.

AWAKENING

Truth will find a way; it may come softly as the dawn steals away the darkness of the night without making a sound and quietly the birth of a new day is born. Not in the same moment will each person turn their face towards the light of truth, but eventually all will journey home.

The awakened mind doesn't judge or condemn. To those who have touched the hem of truth, all religions have relevance and meaning and are but man's attempt to clothe an understanding of God in the rich tapestry of love. If you remove the blinds of separation one truly sees. The mind once awakened perceives the universe anew through the lens of wholeness.

ANGER

Never allow the flame of anger to extinguish the light of your inner peace. If someone directs their anger towards you, try not to add fuel to the fire. Non-action is the greatest action and with no more fuel the fire will eventually burn itself out. Learn to look behind the anger to the need and allow the healing waters of understanding to restore peace.

BEAUTY

A flower does not exist for itself alone. It never realises its own beauty. It exists to remind each one of us, of our own divine beauty. In the moment it exists it is perfect. Its perfection existed within the seed of potentiality, before it blossomed into expression. Awaken to the realisation that you need do nothing other than be yourself, you do not exist for yourself alone, but to serve to be a reminder to all whom you meet of the divine beauty of God.

Beauty is not in things but in each of us by the measure that we have the capacity to perceive the divine in all life, for true beauty is in the look that beholds for it exists as the deepest essence of the soul. We cannot see outside ourselves what we do not already have within. For you are both sunrise and sunset and all the glories and wonders of creation.

BIRTH

A baby is born clothed in the breath of heaven, the delight in remembering the innocence expressed by their presence serves to be a reminder of the love each soul brings as an offering to the world. A child's capacity to experience joy, the ability to perceive magic and wonder in the ordinary, in the very moment a child is born all the earth is born anew

BLESSING

May the gentle earth soften your, footsteps as you walk.

May the grasses and meadows release the fragrance of bright dreams

Which have long been buried in your soul.

May you always remember to nourish the roots of your being

To enable your soul to blossom into becoming

For within you the unknown becomes known

The invisible made visible.

As the ocean is at one with the wave and the wave softly kisses the shore, there is no separation, as night and day belong to each other, you and I are one. Only when you view life from fragmentation do you fail to recognise you are part of this one whole. You are born of the one breath of the eternal and it is written in your heart.

Illuminate our heart and mind,

From both within and without

Dispel all impure thoughts

So, the sweet nectar of love

May infuse our being with the fragrance of the divine.

CHANGE

Life is full of beginnings and endings, what is new will become worn, who is young becomes old, day becomes night and night becomes day again, just as winter flows into spring. All life is constantly experiencing the movement of change. To learn the art of being flexible, to be able to bend with the wind and move with the rhythm of life, means the tension which resistance creates will not cause you suffering, and you will be at peace with your soul through the changing circumstances of life.

CREATION

Can you perceive the magic in creation the majesty of a sunrise, the sweetness of the birdsong? If you cannot then look again so you may be touched by the glory of the universe. Do not die to the world with your life not truly lived, your love unexpressed, your song not sung, your music still in you.

COMMUNICATION.

Every time you endeavour to communicate with those in the eternal world. Create a sacred space in your own being. Clear away the mental debris and clutter created by your material life and your analytical mind.

Ask yourself what gift you bring to the unifying of heaven and earth. Do you bring the gift of your trust and the liberator of belief, free of the limitations created by doubt? For with your loving intent, you create a power which enables those in the eternal world to be at one with you, for a fleeting moment your soul will remember the sweet fragrance of joy, glimpse eternity and bask in the light of truth. So those who some thought dead may speak once more.

DEATH

The autumn leaves that jewel the ground know the art of dying, as they kiss goodbye to the life they once knew, and the tree which freely gave the gift of being. The leaves do not cling or hold on, they know nothing other than how to surrender to the rhythm of nature. Yet by the grace of letting go provide nourishment for the new growth in the spring, people are no different from the leaves of the trees for in dying find new life.

Many people ponder about the possibility of life after death, but there is no after or before - just life!

EMOTIONS

Your emotional states are just your visitors in the guise of emotion. They enter through the door of your mind and they take their departure through the same door. How long they are your guest is entirely up to you. If you dwell in the house of your spirit you will not entertain these false guests who cause you so much suffering and anxiety, alternatively if you dwell in the house of the ego you will always be disturbed and never be at peace. Know, within every given moment of each day, inwardly and energetically you participate in the grace and act of making a choice, regarding the life you choose to live.

ETERNITY

On the shores of Eternity we shall meet you and I, beyond the illusion of self, empty of the opinions which separate one from the other, the walls that divide. On the shores of Eternity we shall meet you and I and realise we are one.

FEAR

Three thieves knocked on the door of self. One was called fear, the second self-doubt, the third denial. Because fear knocked on the door it allowed doubt and denial to enter in and to steal away self-worth, inner peace and recognition of mankind's own divinity. Because of these three thieves', humanity lost all trust in his own self, his neighbour and in the truth that the earth was his garden. So, he listened no longer to the voice of love but to that of fear and ruled by a power which created a hunger caller greed.

Be careful who knocks upon the door of self and what thoughts you let enter in. Never allow fear to steal away the realisation of the love that you are and all you are destined to be.

FLEXIBILTY

If you gaze at the form of you your hands, no finger is the same length, yet if you bend your hands all fingers appear to be equal; even differences can be overcome by movement and flexibility.

GENTLENESS

Never underestimate the power of gentleness. Look at the softness of the first flowers of the year. Even within the icy grip of winter they push through the hard earth, just to remind us that spring is near. In our darkest moments when we feel imprisoned by the frozen emotion of grief, growth moves both gently and silently.

GIVING

Just as the warmth of the sun's rays gently encourages the unfolding of the petals of a flower, so too do praise and encouragement nurture the unfolding of the power of the soul into fullness of expression. As the sun is never the lesser for having given of itself, the one who freely gives is always the richer.

GOD

God the divine musician plays the symphony of love on the strings of our hearts, in the eternal melody of life.

GRACE

The fragrance of transience permeates each life, just as the sun gives life to the morning dew, but for a short while. Ours then, is the glory of the moment, the good deed freely given, the kiss of grace, the laughter, the love unconditionally shown, these things shall shine in the eternal places of heaven's home.

GROWTH.

As the gardener lovingly plants the seed in the darkness of the earth, then tenderly nurtures its growth into being, those in the eternal world devotedly watch over every soul. Growth cannot be rushed as nature takes care of its own, if you try to force open the petals of a flower prematurely it will destroy its natural beauty and form, likewise you cannot hasten spiritual growth and development. At the right time the flower will blossom, and the fruit shall be born to provide nourishment for those who hunger for spiritual truth.

HAPPINESS

Happiness is not in things but in us, when we move beyond the idea that happiness can be found. There is nowhere to seek happiness, the birds never leave behind a footprint in the vast space of the sky, their passage of flight never leaves a trace. Happiness cannot be bought, not even another person can bring you happiness unless it is first realised within.

HEART

Even though your heart may stop beating, and the breath within dissolves like the early morning mist it does not mean you will die, for that which is invisible to the eye can never age or die.

ILLUSION

The three great illusions are power, wealth and fame. There are many people who hunger after power, whether it be power by control of another or a nation; the only power one can ever truly have is, over oneself. The second illusion is wealth. So often people spend their whole lives in the attainment of wealth, mistakenly thinking once they have wealth it will bring in its trail happiness, only to discover that happiness escapes them in the anxiety that they still need more and discover they have lost the most precious thing of all - their life. The third illusion is fame, many people desire to be famous, even amongst religious and spiritually minded people; they hunger for recognition and are governed by the ego. To never want to be anyone other than yourself or arrive anywhere other than where you are right now, enables an inner freedom that wealth, power or fame can never bring.

INVESTMENT

Investing in your own self is the greatest investment you can ever make.

If you had to go on a journey to a foreign country and were limited to what you could fit into a small case, you would take only what was essential to your well-being. Imagine your life is like this case and you can only take with you soul qualities essential to who you are and that are beneficial to your journey. You would never dream of wasting valuable space by filling the case with anything other than what would serve you well. Life is like this, why waste and burden yourself with unnecessary baggage, such as resentment, anger, fear or regret. Leave them behind and travel lightly, learn to value the eternal qualities; to nourish good relations with people you are blessed to share your life with, friendships, love, gratitude, honesty and kindness. for the qualities you have cultivated in this life will clothe your soul in the life to come.

INVISIBLE

You are the invisible within the visible, in the beauty and symmetry of human form you have been born into the world, yet as hard as you may try, you cannot see the soul or that which animates the physical self, just as you cannot see love but instead feel or experience love. Love, like the soul, is invisible but without either you would fail to exist. Within all life it is the invisible which contains the mystery of the divine power that gives birth to the real.

IMPERMANENCE

For a moment the sun gives life to the morning dew as it clings to each blade of grass and for a while myriad colours glisten, only to evaporate in the heat of the day. In spring the trees are bright with cherry blossom just for a brief time, for as soon the rain or winds come the blossom is shaken from the trees. If it were longer would we value the beauty so, for our eyes would soon become accustomed to such a sight.

Impermanence then gives meaning and value to life. Learn to treasure each precious moment and put living into your life, by being the very best you can be. So, God is fulfilled in you as the blossom is fulfilled in its beauty.

LOVE

Love has no bounds, for if it does have limits, it is not love! Do not label or place conditions on your love but allow love to be as a bird and to fly wherever its joy moves it. A bird has wings to soar and the gift to look upon the earth from a vast height, so that in the expression of song it may carry the sweetness of all it beholds to feed the soul of man.

The sun, just by being itself, has the power to melt the most frozen ground and the deepest of snow, by its light and warmth it dissolves that which is frozen and hard. Just as the light of love can dissolve the hardest of hearts, the darkest of fears; we must just let love in.

Love is not an emotion but a quality of the soul, it is not human but divine. As your heart beats within you so too does the pulse of love move through your being. Love exists not in time but in eternity. It is the whole meaning and purpose of existence.

LIGHT

Who can see the stars in the brightness of the sun? The stars have not gone anywhere, their light is simply overpowered by the luminosity of the sun. The stars still exist although not visible. Just as the physical body may die but the spirit lives on and ignorance fades in the light of awareness.

If you light a candle and hold it up to the light of the midday sun its light would be lost, yet in a darkened room the light of even one flame will eradicate the darkness. Because of darkness, light has a name and can be defined, yet darkness does not really exist, it is merely the absence of light. Just as fear is really the absence of love. The soul being born to the world of form may come to recognise its own true nature. Many people say they do not believe in God because they cannot see God, yet the power of God expresses itself in multiplicity, through countless forms of expression, there is nowhere God is not.

MEDIUMSHIP

Never doubt the purpose of your mediumship. One light becomes brighter when it merges with another light, like two candles brought together, its flame becomes a brighter flame.

ONE

Can you separate the in breath from, the out breath,

The wave from the ocean,

The seed from the flower

Night form day

Life from death

All is really one.

PEACE

May you never rest from a deep commitment to be a source of peace in the world. Allow your mind to become as a clear prism through which the light of your inner radiance may shine. Bringing clarity illuminating all things, may your life be the embodiment of truth.

Anything that costs you your peace of mind is too expensive. Learn to travel lightly, put down the burden of your doubts and fears for they are as stones you carry upon your back which weigh you down and delay your progress in life. The past has gone, and the future has not arrived, learn to live so the present does not become tainted by your inability to let go of what is no longer. No matter how hard you may try you cannot change the past, but you can change how you perceive it, if your gaze reflects the light of understanding and your heart is full of love.

PURPOSE

May the nectar of divine grace and love nourish the spirit within, just as the bee pollinates the blossom so the fruit may be borne. May the fruits of the spirit become as food for those who hunger for a deeper meaning, a divine purpose.

PRAYER

True prayer is the soul turned inward, where we gaze through the window of silence to perceive the self. Prayer lives in that which is unspoken within us, it is the act of grace unfolding as the bird spreads its wings before it takes flight.

REASON

Always employ the voice of reason, the sweetness of respect and deep reverence for the sacredness of all life.

REMEMBRANCE

Every time someone in the eternal world is remembered, by a loved one still on earth, the essence of memory fills the heavenly spaces and is received by those, to whom the thought of love is sent. Like incense tapers, that softly rise and make a heavenward ascent, your love moves unseen, yet leaves its fragrance in the soul of those blessed to be remembered still.

RICHES

Who is rich? He who has everything, or he who, having nothing, desires nothing? When you can live beyond the worldly desire to continually fill your empty spaces with more material possessions, you will discover the inner treasures of the spirit.

SEED

You cannot force someone to believe the reality of life eternal if inwardly they are not ready to receive the truth, yet you must never underestimate the potential power of planting a seed. You may never experience the wonder of the flower but know that just to have planted a seed of possibility is sometimes enough.

SELF-REALISATION

As the bee is drawn to the sweet nectar of a flower, as the moth to the flame, and the newly born babe to the comfort of the loving embrace of the arms of its mother, within mankind is a desire to know his own self through God realisation. To awaken to the revelation of the sanctity of all life, God must first be realised within before being realised without. Then and only then will there be a spiritualisation, a quickening of his inherent nature and a recognition of the oneness of all life.

SILENCE

The inactivity of silence encourages the divine activity of awakening. If you cannot sit at peace with your own self, without an inner mental restlessness then progression along the spiritual path may be slow. In every religious tradition there is devotion to the space which exists within silence. Look at the trees in winter, how apparently very little is happening, you see the outer form and fail to perceive the silent quickening of the power that will express itself in the beauty of the leaves in the spring. A majestic offering and testimony to how inactivity and silence give birth to awakening.

What food is to the body, silence is to the soul. For it not only nourishes the inner self but also enables the development of clarity and insight; nearly all the problems created by mankind, the stresses and strains, are brought about by neglecting to nourish the soul in the temple of silence.

Every thought we think or word we say is formed in the womb of silence and is born in the depth of our being from the eternal stillness which exists in every soul.

SPIRIT

You don't need to climb the highest mountain or travel to a distant shore or sit at the feet of a spiritual guru, for the inner self knows no bounds. The entering of the door of a man-made temple will not quicken the pulse of the power of one's own inner spirit, if you have never entered through the door of self and inwardly touched silence.

213

Spirit is the one source and soul of all existence, both seen and unseen. Spirit is the primary cause; because of spirit, matter awakens from the sleep of inertia. Through the living expression of matter, the dawning of consciousness can be realised and the miracle of life itself be known.

Let the spirit of love rinse through your soul and cleanse all your sorrows. Have joy in your life not because of what you have but because of who you are.

May the articulation of your presence be a living prayer, beyond words by the grace of your being. From the light in your eyes, the warmth of your smile, and the love in your heart. Not the reciting of repetitious words, which is as dust which rises in the air just to fall again but the liberating of the silent voice of your soul in true devotion is prayer.

Try not to separate your spiritual nature from your material existence. For your efforts to spiritualise everything you do should flow freely through your life, just as the river flows through the landscape bringing to all the earth the gift of life. Allow the spiritual power within you to nourish all whom you meet, with the blessings of the pure waters of love. The river reaches its destination in the sea, so too will every soul achieve its inevitable goal, merging with the infinite ocean of God's love and be free.

SPEECH

May you speech always flow from a pure heart, allow time for your spirit to rest in the silence of the heart, so your words will not be empty but full of the wisdom of the divine. In every word the song of God, the breath of love.

SPRING

In every falling leaf the sigh of a future spring.

SOUL

On being asked is there a difference between soul and spirit, the answer was, 'spirit is the love and essence of God and soul is the individualised love and essence of God'.

SUFFERING

You were not born to suffer, you suffer because you identify with the ego, rather than the spirit. For the spirit is beyond all emotional states created by the concept of joy and pain, happiness and sadness. Who or what is suffering. Align yourself to the still pool of peace and calm, the waters of love that wash away all falsity. One day happy the next day sad. Learn to dwell in the very centre of your being and not to be bandied about by the ever-changing opinions of others, by circumstance. Smile the sweet smile of knowing and let the grace of god into your house so that all suffering and illusion may be swept away by the breeze of awareness and truth.

STILLNESS

Stand still for a moment, can you not see you are standing on holy ground, everywhere and everything is an expression of love, of God made manifest. Show me where God is not; the life-giving air you breathe, the warm sun, the movement of the tide, the majestic rhythm of the planets, the birth of galaxies, the crops which nourish your physical form, the birds that take flight on wings of grace, the cry of a newly born baby - all is sacred, all is divine. If you fail to see it as such, it is because layer by layer you have immersed yourself in the world of materialism and it has become a distraction to your spirit. Look again at the cosmic dance of life and listen so you can hear the music of God's voice.

TEACHING.

When a person teaches from their soul the benefits are endless. The person they teach is in turn touched by the power of wisdom and they too, being so inspired, will teach others. So the unbroken chain of wisdom softly flows from soul to soul from time to eternity.

THOUGHTS

Thoughts like autumn leaves are blown through silence to the great beyond.

TRANSFORMATION

Just as winter transforms the landscape, so too does pain strip the soul bare as you become exposed to the elements of suffering and are revealed clothed only in your original nature. So that when the springs comes you emerge born anew. Nature reveals herself over again, adorned in a thousand new garments; how many times must you die a death to the old self, before you discover who you really are.

Even stone yields to the rhythm of water constantly beating upon its surface. So it is with each of us, the constant application of right-thinking will ultimately create a channel for the transformation of consciousness.

TRANQUILLITY

Have you ever observed the sea in a storm? How the turbulence of the wind, commands the movement of the waves, to leap and rise, only to crash and fall.Yet beneath the surface, rests undisturbed tranquillity, the life forms that inhabit the depths of the ocean are unaware of the turmoil upon the surface.

The relentless movement and pounding of the waves, represent the problems and difficulties which touch the lives of all, no-one is exempt. Yet if you learnt to rest a while and turn your attention within, you may experience the stillness of your inner spirit, unaffected by the passing waves of anxiety and the dramas of existence; just as the storm will not last forever, all that troubles you so, will one day, also pass.

TRUST.

The birds migrate on wings of trust. They have no earthly map to chart their direction by, only the internal compass, the invisible power which has given the very breath of existence to all life. Be like the birds and trust that the creator of all things, both seen and unseen, resides within your soul.

You need do nothing other than align yourself with your own internal compass to take flight in the direction of trust to find your destiny. Know that this great power will not fail you.

TRUTH.

You are the truth you have been searching for all along, deep within your being lies buried the treasure of remembrance of your true nature, the eternal self. Within the tightly closed shell of the oyster lies the pearl of awakening dive deep into the still waters of the spirit that you find the hidden treasure within. This is unlike any earthly treasure for this jewel of realisation can transform your life forever.

Truth exists whether people choose to realise the truth or not, for truth is not a prisoner of belief, even if no one were to believe in life beyond physical death, it would not, for one moment, stop the reality that life goes on. Life does not begin when you are born to the physical world and neither shall you cease to exist just because your heart has stopped beating. You do not doubt the sun because for a while it is obscured from view, just because you cannot see the eternal world with your eyes does not stop its existence.

UNION

As the river loses its identity as it finds its homecoming in the sea, so does every soul experience the ultimate joy of remembering its true nature in blending with the infinite ocean of God's love.

VALUE.

Empty handed we are born into the world and barefoot we shall leave. Life does not belong to us we belong to life. How you spend each day by the living of your life is important. Do not waste one precious moment for it will never come around again. For even though the seasons return each year, there always exists a variation in the expression of nature. A different countenance of colour and new growth. The greatest sorrow is the unlived life. Learn to value every person you meet, every experience you encounter. You come with nothing other than the gift of yourself and what you take with you will not be any earthly treasures but the perfume of memory, of times spent in the presence of those you love. Mark well the passing of the years and to each person your life has been blessed to touch. Leave behind the sweet remembrance of your love.

VISION

Hold a vision of those you love in your heart and mind, even though they may have left behind the shell of the body, those who truly love can never be apart. They do not belong only to the past but, in the grace of every moment, they exist now, within the shining love of memory and in a future together not yet born.

WONDER

Open the door of wonder that you may enter the inner room of the divine.

WORLD.

You perceive the world through the windows of your mind, cleanse the lens by which you perceive all things. Look through the eyes of love. Do not allow life to cloud your perception but learn to view everybody and situation as an opportunity for growth. So, you may come to realise life reflects to you the beauty of your own soul. Learn to cultivate a beautiful mind an understanding heart

People may know your name

Recognise the contours of your face,

How each line has a story to tell

But no one ever knows the inner world you inhabit,

The bright dreams cherished

How your thoughts colour the experience of each new day

The wounds of the soul are invisible, no one perceives the inner scars

The echoes of longing to be understood behind the walls

Created by opinions and judgments often wrongly made.

Except that is for those in the eternal world

Who hear the sound, of your soul and know your brokenness

And the fleeting butterfly of your joys.

Realise that in those moments when you feel that life has forsaken you.

Benevolent beings keep your company walk beside you

Scattering petals of love to soften your footsteps as you walk

Even though you may deny us, we will never deny you

Even though you may through the mists of time forget us,

we will never forget you

For you and I are one as night and day belong to each other

And the wave which softly kisses the shore belongs to the sea.

SPIRIT TEACHINGS.

THE PIONEER.

It is best to never care to label who you are or who you are not, what you believe or do not believe. Thoughts such as this can create a limitation in the soul's ability to comprehend truth and only serve to create a separation between you and another. Rather than say you are a spiritualist, say, "I follow the way of the spirit". As the spirit by its very nature is free, you will enable yourself to experience freedom. Many people call themselves spiritualists yet fail to seek to work towards spiritualising and enriching their soul and there are others who say nothing of labels yet have been touched by the spirit and have transformed their lives.

Surely the purpose of religion is to awaken within you the voice of truth and to render the divine more visible through the rising perfection of love. To truly know what love is, can be said to be the whole mystery and purpose of human existence. Material achievement, unless it has been to the benefit of mankind in some way, pales into insignificance compared with the ability to know and show love.

In the spirit realities, the soul retains all experiences necessary to facilitate continued growth and equally erases anything that is too painful to bear or recall. This pulsates as a beat of energy within and grants each an ability to understand various qualities of soul and facets of experience.

Each soul is recognised by the pulse of their being and inner vibration, even though their outer form may have changed; this is called soul recognition and like a magnetic force draws one to another, just as kindred spirit whilst upon earth experience an unconscious recollection and familiarity.

Swiftly, within the blink of an eye, memories those on earth have long forgotten are recalled with great ease, as we are not impeded by the limitations that affect us whilst living in the physical form. Therefore memory, which is often attributed only to specific parts of the brain and the function of neurotransmitters, is a condition of the soul. If it were only a function of the brain would memory survive bodily death?

Much of our thinking has become ingrained into our being, as patterns become crystallised energetically and generations of indoctrinated and outworn beliefs are difficult to erase. The process happens gradually, so as not to cause a shock to the vibration of the self; the experience of dying awakens in our physical self the eternal memory of the soul's original nature, the song of life. Everything that is unnecessary or fails to serve our highest objectives begins to fade away and a refinement of soul begins to take place. Eternal progress is a creative possibility for all, none are excluded, no matter the quality of life lived in the material world.

Some might ask what, then, of the law of cause and effect, of compensation and retribution, but life has its own reward. We meet ourselves in many disguises in life through the circumstances which present themselves and our actions cause reactions in the cosmic dance of existence.

On being freed from the bond with the physical body, an expansion in awareness is experienced. It is as though time speeds up and our entire earthly journey moves across the screen of our consciousness, within this process the soul is frequently filled with remorse for any act of selfishness or unkindness and the pain that our actions may have afflicted upon the heart of another is encountered momentarily within oneself. This has mistakenly been called judgement. Nevertheless, it is more accurate to describe such an experience as realisation. It is as though there is a process of coming to terms with oneself; the consequences of such are an immediate desire to make amends in order to progress.

Material existence blinkers us and often it becomes easy to forget the soul's true calling and the truth is that all are part of one vast whole. The giving of a life in service to others brings about an acceleration of soul powers, enabling greater agility between dimensions and within realities.

Only by layers of deep emotional grief are we temporarily separated from you in our abilities to reach you. The energy created by intense grief and loss is extremely dense and can be likened to wading through mud. It is much more conducive when remembering someone you love to have joy in your heart and a smile on your lips. Even though realistically this can be incredibly hard, it facilitates the communication and creates a path of light, likened to a currency of energy which draws us towards it.

Efforts to communicate with those in the spirit realities are made easier by not trying too hard, by not having a fixed predisposition in your mind, desiring a specific outcome. The vibrations of your thoughts produce a vitality of their own, but fear creates its own barrier; it is much more beneficial to create an internal atmosphere of inner freedom.

It is important not to rush. Look at the trees that grow more slowly in the forest, such as the oak, yet produce the strongest wood, timber so strong it can even be used to bear the weight of the roof of a house - yet the trees that grow more quickly do not have the same strength and durability. Be diligent in your efforts and learn to enjoy each new stage of growth and all the possibilities this awakens. Inherent in your soul is a deep awareness of the way the power within you will seek expression. The seed of a pine or sycamore does not need to be told how to create the beauty of its form, although invisible to the eye, the silent power within it knows exactly how to respond. Look how the beauty of the forests blanket the earth and serve humankind by the process of photosynthesis, purifying the air each needs in order to survive upon the earth.

The vibration of our thoughts will be experienced by those who have a receptivity in their spirit. Sometimes we communicate with you and you are unaware of our presence, but never is there a hunger within that goes unrecognised by those in the spirit realities and we will always respond. For we focus our intent on what we wish to say and to this end it is best that you allow yourself to simply become receptive, as there already exists in our awareness a concept of what is necessary to convey. We do not require to be told what we should say. For the need of each loved one will differ from another and the nature of the relationship encountered will create its own unique requirement within.

The intelligence of the spirit can sometimes be undermined by the need of the sensitive to be in control; often this can be due to a misplaced feeling that unless they apply a complicated method the result will elude them.

Communication with spirit is a natural ability inherent in humankind and is available to all, although much depends on a person's state of spiritual understanding and evolution before it is recognised as such.

Not everyone who has made their transition will have a need to communicate, for in the spirit reality it is recognised that, in the beat of a heart, we shall be reunited once more on the shores of eternity despite long years passing on your side of life. Time exists in the world of form and is measured by the changing seasons and governed by the hands of a clock and yet time can sometimes appear to pass slowly or quickly; it is relative, depending upon the level of connectedness or joy you are experiencing, for it is only your perception of time that has altered. How often have you experienced the thrill of waiting for something you have been looking forward to only to find that, once the moment arrives, time seems to speed up.

In our realms time does not exist, as such, but is instead measured by spiritual growth and evolution. Our bodies do not experience the process of ageing and beauty is relative to the degree of soul refinement and the power of love upon which the soul has expanded; the more inner radiance the more it shines from your being. So rather than declining in strength advancement, the opposite, is experienced. On Earth youth is associated with beauty and those whose face is lined by the experiences of life are often classed as not so beautiful; this is nothing more than a judgment, predetermined by the conditioned mind, for it is the light of the soul that illuminates the body in true beauty.

There are those in the heavenly realms whose countenance shines and by their very presence fill your own soul with an empowerment, it is not dissimilar to the refreshment you experience when you have a great thirst and take a long, cool drink on a hot summer's day. To be in the presence of these enlightened beings quickens your inner vibration and creates a desire to seek further progression.

Places of great beauty exist where you can receive according to your need, if the need enriches your spiritual self. The gardens are overflowing with flowers both similar and dissimilar to those on earth. Types and varieties which no longer exist upon the physical level, as the environment is no longer conducive, here still enjoy a life. Some gardens are filled in order of various themes of colour where each flows freely into the next, according to shade or hue. Others are as a scattered profusion of light and sound, but it is only those that have developed their sensitivity enough who can perceive the most delicate melodies, for the same dimension may be inhabited by many, each attuned to a different level of perception, according to each individual's stage of awareness. This typically explains why there is an inconsistency in the descriptions relayed through various channels about life in the spirit realities. For you can only experience according to the degree to which you have the capacity to conceive.

Rich and diverse landscapes stretch endlessly into a sense of spaciousness, a certain familiarity exists in comparison with earthly landscapes and yet striking differences occur; it is as though an impression experienced within your mind can change or alter the appearance of things, yet only by virtue of degrees. You may, subject to inner desire, change the colour of a flower as the environment seems to clothe itself in the shape of your thoughts, bringing great comfort to the soul. It is only possible to alter an aspect of something, it is not possible to change your entire surroundings as it is not only your landscape; in truth it belongs to all whilst at the same time being a reflection of the soul's innermost feelings. Trees sound their own inner harmonies and resonance that is possible to hear with the soul. The vibration brings into manifestation new life in a similar way a pine tree on earth each year would shed a seed of potential life; the vibration of sound creates new trees in areas not yet filled with their beauty. The music of one tree can be likened to a soloist singing one song, by comparison a forest can be likened to a grand choir.

Each strata of life comprises its own medley and sound that is reshaping, in constant patterns, new aspects or spheres of existence. When a soul evolves and grows spiritually from a life on earth it takes back to the eternal world an added vibration or energy which fosters the potential for something new and wonderful to be formed.

The longer we inhabit the spiritual realms the more our earthly life begins to fade from our conscious awareness and material existence becomes as a distant dream, until, that is, we draw near your level once more, then it is as though we are momentarily immersed in the recollection of a life once lived. It's not that we choose to forget, as any memory can be recalled instantly if so desired, it's just it becomes less significant.

We are bound always to those we love, and any pain or sorrow encountered vibrates upon the ether, like a musician who on touching the string of a violin with a bow brings life to the instrument and induces the mystical harmonies of sound. Long after the note has sounded, a tender nuance can be felt within the soul.

Our work can be best defined by doing what we love, this is the soul's true calling, and by the expression of whatever innate qualities the soul possesses we will creatively add to the nature of the spirit world or benefit others. A challenge is to imagine something into existence which by its very nature will enhance the surroundings. To think something into reality is not an ability that all have; the art of applying concentrated intent without any distraction is necessary, you must first master the art of imagining and think it into being.

Before anything of value exists upon the earth it is first breathed into life in our world. The blueprint, so to speak, belongs to the spirit reality, as matter is crystalised light. All great works of art and literature are created in the divine imagination and are received by highly creative souls who are receptive to the outpouring of inspiration. Very often the greatest and most timeless of works were experienced in a flash of insight, frequently with rapidity, as in this heightened state spiritual powers of awareness are awakened. The spirit body, not belonging to time or space, exists in eternity.

Great discoveries are ideas received by receptive minds and happen when there is a synchronicity of energy, a harmonising of the right moment and a tapping into a need so that they can be made manifest in the world of form, to the benefit of mankind in some new way. To this end there are those in the spirit realms who are skilled in the art of both directing and relaying a frequency of thought, to the benefit of those on earth, to bring about a quickening in knowledge and new understanding to the advancement of all.

Many people choose to think in concepts such as here or there, dead or alive, but in truth all are one and the same. When we experience the awakened self, we begin to understand in a way which transforms everything. Some find it difficult to conceive of the one life, just as the caterpillar could probably not comprehend life as a butterfly being an aspect of the same existence.

Nothing ever dies, not even the small winged birds that fly; they still fill the atmosphere with song, which is carried through the breeze. What differs is the experience of the birdsong, it is as though there is an understanding of what they are saying, and this is felt within, and gladdens, the spirit. Some qualities that cannot live in your soul in the eternal places are those of negativity or sadness. You may have a momentary longing of some kind, but not sadness, for sadness is not a true condition of the soul.

THE REVELATION OF COMMUNICATION

The desire of the sensitive to communicate quickens their vital body, thus making it easier for those in our world to draw near, creating a pulse of energy through the nervous system that vitalises all levels of being. It is rather like a gentle electrical charge or current, along which the communication is expressed. The information is then transferred, and thus received, at whatever level of awareness is most heightened within the medium. A sensitive really is a conduit for this universal power to move through; just as the riverbed is shaped by the water that flows in a constant stream, so too does our power ultimately create a more distinct and defined channel of communication, the more those in our world use the sensitive.

Eventually a rapport is created which enables a deepening in the quality of the information being both relayed and received. By process of evolution people are developing their spirituality and raising their consciousness so, as every effort is made to be at one, the process is extended. At the speed of light, we relay information through the medium, our thoughts are light energy shaped by our intent and clothed in the form we wish to express. It is no surprise, then, that various information can be simultaneously passed to the soul which is translated via the nervous system. Drawn from the memory contained within the self we transfer significant memories or required information, thus seeing, hearing, tasting and smelling are all recreated by those on our side of life to replicate what it is we desire to convey. For not only is it important to eradicate fear created by ignorance of man's eternal nature from the minds and hearts of those we love, but also to liberate humanities' thinking.

The more a medium purifies his or her thinking, being and living, the more this process of spiritual advancement can be refined. It is not necessary to live an unnatural life, but rather a life which is governed by purity of intent and integrity of spirit. We are born on the earth to experience the richness of the fruits of existence, but also to remember not to neglect the spirit or all that serves as food to nourish the soul.

There is so much scope within the potential of each individual if man but knew that spirit and spirit can meet. It has only been ignorance of reality which has created a wall between your world and ours, separated by perpetual doubt about a life beyond that which you now know. Truly, then, to become more aware is to become free.

Not everyone in the spirit dimensions has a need to communicate, some are content to know that they can be close without ever receiving actual recognition of their presence. As it is necessary for those on this side of life to go through a process where temporarily we are immersed in all the limits of earthly existence, and the pains once suffered, it can be likened to finding a path in a fog. Fear changes the energy around a person and slows down the impulse of communication, so it can become distorted. It is vital that every effort to communicate is accompanied by a loving desire to be of service. Technology is rapidly progressing but at the same time so are the natural qualities within the sensitive. There is every possibility that the whole atomic nature of the individual is speeding up, so that what were once called miracles will become the acceptable norm for generations not yet born. There is nothing outside of natural law and divine order. Even natural catastrophes are the Earth's attempts to correct an imbalance of some kind, invariably from the effect of what has been created by mankind's ignorance. For the Earth itself has a soul and consciousness and all manner of life should be protected and tended to with great love.

To seek the direction from those who have a clearer vision, and a greater breadth of understanding, will enrich the whole. To this end those in the spirit realities work unceasingly and seize every opportunity that serves to inspire another to awaken man from his sleep into the dawn of truth; that you are eternal beings and life by its very nature cannot die

Trance teachings from "The Pioneer"

THESE THINGS SHALL BE, A LOFTIER RACE.

These things shall be a loftier race

Than e'er the world hath known shall rise

With flame of freedom in their souls

And light of knowledge in their eyes

Nation with nation, land with land,

Unarmed shall live as comrades free;

In every pulse and heart shall throb,

The praise of one fraternity.

New arts shall bloom of loftier mould,

And mightier music thrill, the skies,

And every life shall be a song

When all the earth is paradise.

James Addington Symonds.

I am sure it is the deepest wish of those in the spirit world that a new world vision of true brotherhood be established. Particularly during the collective hardships being experienced globally in our present times, it offers mankind an opportunity to direct our awareness away from greed and a society fixated on excess, in order to re-evaluate and re-prioritise what is actually important in our life. In times of crisis, whether personally or globally, life calls to each of us to look not without but within to what really sustains us from the inside.

If you feel that you are strongly drawn to be of service to the spirit world through your mediumistic sensitivities or healing, with all the endless ways of expression that this embodies, remember that every time you turn one person to the light of truth and awareness of man's inherent divinity, you help others to rise above the conditioning of the ages and give freedom to a future generation. For there exist many forms of slavery; ignorance is the greatest chain of all and has been the cause of nearly every violation of the human spirit known to man. Never think that just by bringing a loved one through you have fulfilled your purpose, for within the trail of this there exist vast implications that have the power to not only change the person who is receiving the communication but, potentially, the world.

Realise every time you make an effort to represent the spirit world, that you belong to a vast lineage of great souls, who in their day served humanity. Those who have gone before us were ordinary people, but by virtue of their abilities and measure of all they gave, were also extraordinary; they have invested in you, belief, hope, and trust, in a future generation, upon which you too will also build. Do not falter from this great task, even though at times the road before you may be paved with difficulties, we are never beyond the reach of their outstretched arms and tender care.

Our greatest gift to ourselves, needed at this time in history more than any other, would be to acknowledge that we should all be living in harmony with gratitude that we are all equal participants in the great mystery of life and above all else recognise that, despite all our differences, we belong to each other. For the longest time those who some would refer to as dead have dared to voice this one truth; that the life of one is connected to the life of all. This is our human destiny – to awaken from the fear that has imprisoned us for generations and to learn to love and cherish one another, after all, we are just walking each other home. Beyond the spoken word, in the silencing of thought, we are already there. In truth we always have been, we have just been fooled into thinking otherwise.

May you stand on tiptoes and touch the stars.

Eileen

ACKNOWLEDGMENTS

With gratitude to Anne Harrison for kind permission to quote the wonderful story regarding the mediumship of Minnie Harrison.

FURTHER INQUIRY

Institute of Noetic Sciences website https://noetic.org/

Jose Medrado website www.cidadedaluz.com.br/jose-medrado/ index.html

This book can be purcased from

https://www.eileendavies.com/shop